FEDERER

PORTRAIT OF A TENNIS LEGEND

This edition printed in 2019
by Carlton Books Limited
20 Mortimer Street
London W1T 3JW

A CIP catalogue record for this book is available
from the British Library

ISBN 978-1-78739-240-3

Editorial Director: Martin Corteel
Project Editor: Ross Hamilton
Design Manager: Luke Griffin
Designer: Rockjaw Creative
Picture Research: Paul Langan
Production: Ena Matagic

Printed in Dubai

OPPOSITE: Federer's record-breaking exploits over two remarkable decades on the professional circuit have seen the multiple Grand Slam champion win a worldwide legion of fans.

FEDERER

PORTRAIT OF A TENNIS LEGEND

IAIN SPRAGG

CARLTON
BOOKS

CONTENTS

INTRODUCTION
THE ROGER FEDERER STORY

An iconic athlete who has transcended his own sport, Federer's remarkable career has been a story of unprecedented success during which the elegant and enduringly popular Swiss has repeatedly rewritten the history of tennis.

"The Greatest" is an epithet in modern sport diminished by its too frequent attribution. Tennis has many claimants to the coveted title but when it is measured by Grand Slam wins, tour titles, Olympic and Davis Cup successes, not to mention incredible longevity and the manner in which it has all been achieved, there is only one undisputed king of the court.

To distil Federer's career into mere statistics and winning percentages is, however, only half the story. No man has won more majors or reached as many Grand Slam finals, spent more weeks at the summit of the world rankings or dominated the game over such a prolonged period. Yet, as encyclopaedic as his myriad achievements undoubtedly are, the Swiss is much more than a statistical phenomenon.

To watch Federer play is a study in style, and in a sport increasingly typified by power and physicality, he has always been an old-fashioned throwback to a bygone era of almost effortless grace and technique. Other players may hit harder and serve bigger but none have been able to rival the Swiss's natural movement, timing and vision on court. It is an approach to the game that has earned him a global legion of fans within tennis and made him one of the most famous sportsmen on the planet.

"He is the most beautiful man to watch play tennis," said John McEnroe. "The most beautiful I've ever seen play. His movement, combined with the artistry, his racket, the look, he's got everything going." The legendary Björn Borg added, "Roger is the greatest player ever who played the tennis game."

Federer's journey to greatness started in the Swiss city of Basel in the early 1980s. Tennis was far from his only childhood sporting love but from the moment at the age of 12 that he decided to devote his energies exclusively to the courts of the Old Boys' Tennis Club in his hometown, rather than the football pitch or ski slopes, the die was cast and a star was born.

What followed was a litany of junior and subsequent senior success. Crowned Wimbledon boys' champion in the summer of 1998, Federer made his professional debut in Switzerland just 24 hours later. Within three years, despite not yet having celebrated his 20th birthday, he claimed his maiden Association of Tennis Professionals (ATP) tour title with victory in Italy in the final of the Milan Indoors tournament. Rising rapidly up the ranks, the teenager then seared his name into the public consciousness when he beat the legendary Pete Sampras, the seven-time Centre Court champion, in five sets at Wimbledon in 2001.

PREVIOUS PAGE: Hendam The Swiss' natural rapport with tennis fans has epitomised his incredible career as much as his unprecedented haul of trophies and titles.

OPPOSITE: Pictured at the 88th annual Academy Awards in Hollywood, 2016, the elegant Swiss is widely acknowledged as the greatest player the men's game has ever witnessed.

His record-breaking deluge of 20 Grand Slam triumphs began in the summer of 2003 when the Swiss returned to Wimbledon, dispatching the Australian Mark Philippoussis in the final to join tennis's exclusive club of major winners. Federer has reached 29 further finals since his pivotal win in SW19, emerging victorious in 19 of them, and no player in the history of the game has featured in so many. No one has won the Wimbledon men's singles title more than his eight victories at the All England Club and he is also the joint record holder in the modern era with five triumphs at both the Australian and US Opens.

Federer's illustrious career has been one characterized by his love of grass and hard courts but he demonstrated his versatility and brilliance in 2009 when he claimed a maiden French Open title on the clay of Roland-Garros. After winning four majors, the Swiss had become only the sixth player – and the first in 20 years – to complete the fabled career Grand Slam.

His record beyond the four majors is equally staggering. An Olympic gold medallist after winning the men's doubles title with compatriot Stan Wawrinka at the 2008 Games in Beijing, he also led Switzerland to Davis Cup glory for the first time in 2014, defeating France in the final in Lille. His haul of six end-of-season ATP World Tour Finals successes is another stand-alone record while the total of 310 weeks he has bestrode the men's world rankings is a milestone that may never be eclipsed.

Federer turned 36 in 2017 but in contrast to other athletes of his vintage competing in an unforgiving, physically intense sport, the great man's powers and hunger for trophies were undimmed. He had gone almost five years without a Grand Slam win but proved that while form is fleeting, class is permanent with victory in the final of the Australian Open and then at Wimbledon, becoming the oldest Centre Court champion of the Open Era.

He was triumphant once again in Melbourne the following year proving that his extraordinary

career was far from finished. His progress to the final in Australia was the 19th season in succession the Swiss had reached the climax of an ATP tournament.

The Federer story, of course, cannot continue

forever. He has remained relatively injury free during his two decades on the professional circuit, while his ability to glide across the court has been less attritional on the body than many of his contemporaries who have long since retired. But there will inevitably come a day when the Swiss finally turns his back on the sport which he has so stylishly redefined. All those who love tennis can only hope that day does not come soon.

ABOVE: Federer's triumph at Wimbledon in 2017, beating Marin Cilic in straight sets, was the 19th Major of his career and a record eighth title at the All England Club.

THE BOY FROM BASEL

1

THE BOY FROM BASEL

Years before global fame and fortune beckoned, Federer grew up in the unassuming Swiss city of Basel, dividing his childhood between school, tennis courts, Alpine ski slopes and his local video arcade.

Roger Federer was yet to celebrate his fourth birthday in the summer of 1985 when Boris Becker made worldwide headlines with his historic victory in the Wimbledon final. The unseeded German teenager was just 17 years, seven months and 15 days old when he defeated Kevin Curren in four sets on Centre Court in SW19, becoming the youngest player ever to lift the game's most coveted trophy.

The three-year-old Swiss was too young to remember anything of Becker's era-defining triumph that day. His earliest tennis memory is watching the charismatic German on television as he lost to Swede Stefan Edberg in the Wimbledon final three years later. Becker's infectious, all-action style still made an indelible impression on Federer and, like many of his generation, he grew up idolizing the player affectionately dubbed "Boom Boom". Few, however, would have envisaged that he would eventually eclipse the achievements of his childhood hero.

"I was told by my parents that I cried about the outcome of that final," he told *The Times* in a 2005 interview. "The reason? My first sporting hero, Boris Becker, had been beaten. To a six-year-old, defeat seemed so tragic. How was I to know that Becker would go on to win his third Wimbledon title a year later? Or that he would also collect the champion's trophies at the

Australian Open twice and the US Open? Or that five-and-a-half years after he first threw away victory on that most beautiful of tennis lawns, he would finally become the world's number one ranked tennis player?

"Boris was everybody's favourite player. Look at the way he took the sport by surprise. He was just 17 when he won that first title in 1985. Becker's game was immense. It was the era of "Boom Boom" and nobody was able to stand in his way. It was the memory of the three consecutive Becker finals with Edberg [between 1988 and 1990] that set my imagination racing and put me on course to where I am today."

Federer's story – and spectacular rise to the pinnacle of his sport – began in August 1981 when he was born at the Basel Cantonal Hospital, the second child of Robert and Lynette. Robert was a Swiss-German from St Gallen in the north-east of the country. Federer's mother was a South African from the province Gauteng and the pair had met on a business trip to Africa.

His parents were keen amateur tennis players and members of the Ciba Tennis Club, a private club for employees of the Basel-based chemical company where they both worked. A young Federer was a familiar face at the club along with Robert and Lynette and older sister Diana, and by the age of four he was already hitting balls on

the distinctive red clay of the club's courts rather than merely sitting on the sidelines.

"We would go to play tennis and Roger just picked up the racket and started playing," his mother said. "He loved the sport from the beginning. The children have to put their hearts and souls into it. They cannot be forced to do it, not by the mother, the father, the school, or the coach."

Tennis, though, was not Federer's only love when growing up. Badminton, basketball, squash and table tennis all caught his attention and he also played for the Concordia Basel football team. He was an accomplished skier and equally at home on the slopes of the Swiss Alps as he was increasingly becoming on the tennis court.

"I remember always loving to play against the garage door, or against the cupboard doors inside, with any kind of ball. My mum got fed up because it was bang, bang, bang all day. I would watch tennis matches on television for hours on end. I liked tennis the best of all sports. It was always exciting, and winning or losing was always in my hands."

Roger Federer

Precocious, innate ability in a wide range of sports at a young age is a familiar theme for those who develop into world-class athletes. Federer's natural hand–eye coordination with any kind of racket in his hand was already evident – but it was to be tennis which ultimately won the battle for his talents when, at the age of six, he was invited to train three times a week with a regional development squad in Basel. It was a move that would set him on his path to sporting greatness.

At these regional sessions, Federer met Marco Chiudinelli, a fellow Basel boy and future Davis Cup teammate, and they quickly became friends. The young duo would head to the Steinenvorstadt district of the city and their favourite arcade to indulge their shared passion for video games. The pair first found themselves on opposite sides of the net in a competitive event at the age of eight when they were drawn against each other in the "Bambino Cup" in Arlesheim.

"Back then, we only played one long set of up to nine games," Chiudinelli said. "Things weren't going well for me at the beginning. I was behind 2-5 and I started to cry. We cried a lot back then, even during the matches. Roger came up to me and tried to comfort me when we switched sides. He told me everything would be all right, and in fact, things got better. I took the lead 7–6 and noticed that the tide had turned.

"Then he began to cry and I ran up to him, gave him encouragement and things went better for him. It was the only time I could beat him. I could give him a thrashing in training but when we played in a tournament a day later, he gave me a thrashing. Even back then, he was a real competitor. When it came down to business, he could flip a switch and become a completely different person. I admired that about him."

In the same year that Federer competed in the Bambino Cup, he bid farewell to Ciba and joined a new club, Old Boys in Basel. The switch brought him into contact with the club's resident head professional Adolf Kacovsky and, by the age of 10, he was receiving weekly, one-to-one coaching from the man better known to members as "Seppli". The youngster made an immediate impression on Kacovsky when they worked together on Court Five, the furthest from the clubhouse.

"I noticed right away that this guy was a natural talent," Kacovsky said. "He was born with a racket in his hand. The club and I quickly realized he was enormously talented. We began giving him private lessons that were partly funded by the club. Roger was a quick learner. When you wanted to teach him something new, he was able to pick it up after three or four tries, while others needed weeks. I would tell him how to hit a shot and he would get it straight away. Roger always had dreams of being a professional tennis player. He would tell me that he was going to become the world number one. I've coached for over 40 years and never seen such a gifted player. Roger was exceptional even then. I thought that he would perhaps become the best player in Switzerland or Europe but not the best in the world. He had it in his head and he worked at it."

Federer's commitment was evident in 1993 when, at the age of 12, he hung up his football boots to focus exclusively on tennis. In the same year he had what was to be his first encounter with tennis royalty when he was chosen to be a ballboy at the Swiss Indoors championship at the St. Jakobshalle arena, a 30-minute walk from the family home in the Wasserhaus area of Basel.

The final of the tournament saw Germany's Michael Stich, the 1991 Wimbledon champion, play Edberg, then a five-time Grand Slam winner. The Swede had already claimed the Basel title three times in his career but was denied a quartet of triumphs as Stich blasted his way to a four-set victory. Tradition dictated that the new champion present each of the ballboys and girls a medal to mark the occasion. Images of Federer meeting the victorious German were to prove a prophetic precursor of the meteoric career the youngster was about to embark on.

Federer was back at the Swiss Indoors in 1994 to resume his ballboy duties. Four years later, he walked through the doors of the St Jakobshalle as a player, facing Andre Agassi in the first round in front of his partisan home crowd. A certain Boris Becker also happened to be among the 32-strong field of competitors.

CLIMBING THE JUNIOR RANKS

2

CLIMBING THE JUNIOR RANKS

Now in his formative and frequently volatile teenage years, Federer took a life-changing decision to move away from his family and friends in Basel to pursue his dreams of forging a career in professional tennis.

It was a big year for Roger Federer in 1993. His stint as a ballboy at the Swiss Indoors in his hometown had presented him with the opportunity to watch some of the game's greats at close quarters. Those charged with nurturing his development, however, were more concerned with the youngster's own game and progression. As the years passed, Federer did not disappoint them.

In 1993, the 12-year-old won two Swiss national titles to underscore his burgeoning potential and, by the time he was 14, he had been crowned Switzerland's junior champion and had reached the quarter-finals of the prestigious Orange Bowl in Key Biscayne, Florida. Federer now had an embryonic reputation in Swiss tennis circles but the next stage of his career was to prove initially painful.

In 1995, he was invited to attend the Swiss Tennis Academy in Ecublens near Lausanne, a 120-mile drive south from Basel. The move would require leaving the family home for five days a week and his family feared the 14-year-old would suffer from homesickness. Federer, however, knew the chance to train with and compete against the country's best players was one he could not refuse.

"We are a close family, but Roger took the decision at a very early age that he wanted to play tennis away from home," his mother Lynette said. "We never forced him to do anything, we let him develop on his own. He made a lot of important decisions himself when he was younger and that was key to his success because he had to learn how to do things for himself. He learned to be very independent.

His parents organized a family holiday to Australia before he packed his bags but, before long, the teenager was commuting between Basel and his adopted second family, the Christinets, with whom he lodged in Ecublens. "I remember one wonderful trip with my parents back when I was 14, before I entered the tennis centre, one big trip all the way to Australia," he said. "I travelled the East Coast with my sister and parents, going to Sydney, Queensland, Cairns and also the Great Barrier Reef. After that, my life sort of changed and I became much more serious as a professional with tennis. From 14 to 16, I would leave at 6 p.m. on Sundays and come back on Fridays, playing tournaments a two-hour train ride away, in the midst of people taking the train back and forth to work."

Federer's enforced relocation brought challenges for the young teenager as he struggled to adapt to life away from his parents and sister, as well as the language barrier he faced travelling from a German-speaking area of Switzerland to a French-speaking one.

"When he left us to go to Ecublens, it was a torment," said Madeleine Barlocher, who was in

LEFT: The Swiss Under-18 champion at the age of 16, Federer's growing reputation was further enhanced when he won the prestigious Torneo Internazionale Città di Prato in Italy in 1997.

charge of the junior programme at the Old Boys club in Basel. "He was adored by everyone. It was difficult also for him. His mother told me that, for the entire first month there, he didn't do anything but cry."

That inner emotional steel that would later in his career become a hallmark on court helped see him through this period of teenage upheaval and change. His friendship with Yves Allegro, three years his senior fellow Ecublens squad member and future Davis Cup cohort, was another significant factor in Federer successfully adapting to his new life.

Now feeling increasingly more settled, the youngster's burning ambition to become a world-class, rather than journeyman, player became more and more apparent to those around him. "We had to compile a questionnaire to indicate our goals," recalled Allegro. "Everyone dreamed to break into the Top 100, but only Roger wanted to break into the Top 10 and become world number one. We all saw that only he understood that he was improving much and that he thought to do important things."

There was, though, a major problem. The Federer of today may be the epitome of cool, calm composure but in his teenage years he struggled with a far more volatile temperament that he was unable to control and which led to on-court outbursts, tantrums and meltdowns. He was, in truth, the antithesis of the man millions of tennis fans would come to idolize.

"It was so funny when Roger won Wimbledon for the first time [in 2003] and then started crying," said coach Barlocher. "I remember when he was little and lost a match, and he would try to hide behind the umpire's chair, and would not stop crying for more than 10 minutes. The next time I saw Roger after that, I said to him, 'You used to cry when you lost a match, and now you cry when you have won a match.' Roger laughed when I reminded him of that."

Federer's mother was equally aware of her son's tendency to become overwhelmed by what happened on court. "This stage was part of his growing up," she told the *Telegraph* in an interview in 2005. "But when his behaviour was bad, we told him that it was bad and that it

upset us. We used to say, 'Come on, Roger, get control of yourself, pull yourself together.' He says that he can't remember crying when he played tennis, but he also cried when he played football. I remember saying to him once, 'Is it such a catastrophe if you lose a match?' But the tears just showed how ambitious Roger was, how determined he was to succeed."

Tears may have been one thing but it was his tantrums that gave his inner circle more cause for concern. He once earned himself a week-long punishment cleaning toilets after ripping a courtside curtain with a racket he had thrown in a fit of pique at a training camp. By his own admission, Federer was something of an enfant terrible before he learned to control his emotions.

"I had a tough time getting my act together out on court, trying to behave properly," he said. "For me, that was a big deal. I was throwing around my racket like you probably don't imagine. Helicopters were flying all over. I was getting kicked out of practice sessions non-stop when I was 16, before I started just to relax a little bit more on court. I realized that the racket throwing didn't help my game because I was always getting very negative."

His anger issues continued to be a worry but a perceptible improvement in his behaviour began after he decided to speak to a sports psychologist. "I had one between 1997 and 1998," he said. "It was more like anger management. That was what it was about for me then. I pretty quickly realized it was basically up to me and not someone else to tell me how to behave, because my parents were telling me anyway, friends as well. Other players were saying, 'What is wrong with you?' That was just up to me to decide when I wanted to take that step and say, you know what, let's try the quiet version of Roger Federer."

The more circumspect youngster continued to impress despite his outbursts. In July 1996, he joined the International Tennis Federation's junior circuit and was also crowned the Swiss Under-16 national champion to underline his ongoing improvement. By the end of 1996, he was ranked 86th in the country and, as a result, was promoted to the A-League of Swiss tennis.

The following year saw Federer's already rapid progress achieve breakneck speed. The Swiss Under-18 crown at the age of 16 confirmed his domestic dominance, but it was in May in Italy that he began to extend his reach by winning the prestigious Torneo Internazionale Città di Prato. People outside Switzerland were now beginning to mention him as a possible future senior champion.

It was also in 1997 that the Swiss Federation Tennis School moved from Ecublens, 60 miles north-east to the town of Biel. The switch required Federer to uproot once again but this time, reflecting his growing maturity, his mother and father decided he was old enough to live in private accommodation rather than with a host family. "Roger's parents told me that they would have been happy if their son had shared an apartment with an older player," said his friend and new flatmate Allegro. "They asked me if I was available to do it."

Aside from his living arrangements, the move to Biel had a more fundamental impact on Federer's career as it brought him back into direct contact with Australian coach Peter Carter. A former ATP World Tour player and future Swiss Davis Cup captain, the pair had first met at Old Boys in Basel when Federer was nine. Their reunion would see Carter expertly guide his charge as he took his first, tentative steps in the professional ranks.

As 1997 gave way to 1998, Federer was on the cusp of making his debut in the game's senior professional ranks. Before he crossed the threshold into men's tennis, he found himself in London in late June on the hallowed grass courts of Wimbledon competing in the boys' singles and doubles tournaments. He had already reached the semi-finals of the Australian Open boys' in January and hopes were high that he could go even further in London.

The 16-year-old Swiss was seeded five in the Wimbledon boys' singles and was untroubled in the early rounds as he swept aside Austrian Philipp Langer, Andrej Kracman from Slovenia

OPPOSITE: Federer's meteoric rise up the ranks gathered speed in 1998 when he made his debut in three of the four junior Grand Slam events.

and France's Jérôme Haehnel to reach the quarter-finals. He needed a tiebreak win to overcome Brit David Sherwood in two sets in the last eight before dispatching Croatian Lovro Zovko in the semis. He then tasted what was to be the first of many SW19 triumphs after beating Irakli Labadze from Georgia 6-4, 6-4 in the final. For the first time, Federer was a Wimbledon champion, successfully following in the illustrious footsteps of previous winners of the junior title, such as Stefan Edberg, Pat Cash, Ivan Lendl and Björn Borg. All but Lendl went on to be crowned men's champion later in their careers.

"It feels like it happened yesterday," Federer told the BBC in 2018. "I was very excited to be in the final. It was played back on the old Court Two, where we had our locker room. To be honest, I would have preferred to have played on Centre Court. I remember match point was on my second serve. I was so happy to win, even though I didn't know at the time what it meant for me. I knew it was a big deal and it started my dream of winning the men's title. I am very proud how I was able to carry myself in the final."

Peter Carter was on hand to witness the triumph in London. Although he insisted on keeping a level head about the biggest win of his young charge's career to date, he was in no doubt what had been the deciding factor in the final. "Roger played with the concentration of a professional," he said at the time. "Now he just has to improve his volleys."

However, the teenager was not finished. In the doubles he paired up with Belgian Olivier Rochus and, despite dropping a set in the last eight, the duo ultimately proved unstoppable on the grass and claimed the title with a 6-4, 6-4 victory over Israeli Andy Ram and Michaël Llodra from France in the final.

Victory at Wimbledon opened doors for the teenage prodigy and, as he matured, he began to take these opportunities with increasing regularity. His days in junior tennis were almost behind the Swiss as he set his sights on the daunting and demanding world of the ATP's men's circuit.

"It was a great lesson in life for him – that things don't always go your own way, and that you don't get anywhere in life with talent alone. You have to work at things. I know that it wasn't always fun and games for Roger, and that on many days he wasn't that happy. But those struggles were good for him. Overcoming those ups and downs was a challenge for him, and it helped him to develop as a person."

Lynette Federer *on her son's relocation to the Swiss Federation Tennis School in Ecublens.*

OPPOSITE: Victory in the final of the Wimbledon boys' singles in 1998, beating Irakli Labadze from Georgia, helped propel Federer to number one in the junior world rankings.

PROFESSIONAL PROGRESSION

3

PROFESSIONAL PROGRESSION

Victory in the boys' singles at Wimbledon confirmed Federer as one of the game's hottest young prospects and the teenager was now ready to continue his sporting education against tennis's bigger beasts.

Few would have begrudged Roger Federer some form of celebration after his triumph in SW19. It was, after all, the most notable success of his embryonic career and, while the 16-year-old was still too young to have raised a glass of something sparkling to toast his success, it wouldn't have been inappropriate to have marked the occasion in some way.

In reality, he didn't even make it to the traditional star-studded Champions' Dinner, which was held on the second Sunday of Wimbledon, the same day as Federer's win in the final. Instead, the youngster unexpectedly found himself on a plane headed to his home town of Basel.

The reason for his sudden departure from London was the start of the Swiss Open in Gstaad. The ATP tournament began on the Monday and although his lowly world ranking of 702 was well below the usual requirement for the event, the tournament director decided to hand Federer a wild card for the clay court competition in the wake of his Wimbledon success. Still a month short of his 17th birthday, Federer was about to make his debut in professional tennis.

Germany's Tommy Haas was scheduled to play Federer in the first round but withdrew at the 11th hour due to illness. As a result, Federer played Lucas Arnold, an Argentine clay-court specialist who was ranked 88th in the world. It was to be no fairytale beginning: Federer lost 6-4, 6-4 in front of his home crowd, but Arnold was left in no doubt of the potential of his young opponent. "He plays like Pete Sampras," he said after the match, "and he has a great serve."

Federer himself was disappointed with the result, despite no one having predicted he would beat a vastly more experienced Top 100 player seven years his senior. "I competed very hard, but did not play well," he said. "If I had played well, I would have won. You have to do more running with the professionals than with the juniors and pros are not going to make as many mistakes."

There was, however, no time to dwell on his defeat as by August 1998, he found himself in America competing in the boys' singles at the US Open. He found Flushing Meadows almost as much to his liking as Wimbledon, as he battled through to the final, although he was taken to three sets in both the last eight and last four, but David Nalbandian of Argentina proved too strong for him in the showpiece match and the Swiss went down 6-3, 7-5.

The following month, Federer added another significant entry on his burgeoning CV when he recorded his first-ever victory on the professional tour, beating Guillaume Raoux in the Frenchman's own backyard in the first round of the Grand Prix

de Tennis de Toulouse. In October, he found himself in familiar surroundings, courtesy of another wild card, when he competed in the Swiss Indoors in Basel. He was only able to take five games when he was defeated by the legendary Andre Agassi at St Jakobshalle but the experience gained from facing the multiple Grand Slam winner would prove invaluable.

There were still more significant landmarks for Federer in 1998. In December, he won the Orange Bowl in Florida, the unofficial world junior championship, after beating Guillermo

ABOVE: At the age of 17 Federer graduated to the professional ranks in the summer of 1998 when he featured in the Swiss Open in Gstaad.

PROFESSIONAL PROGRESSION | 31

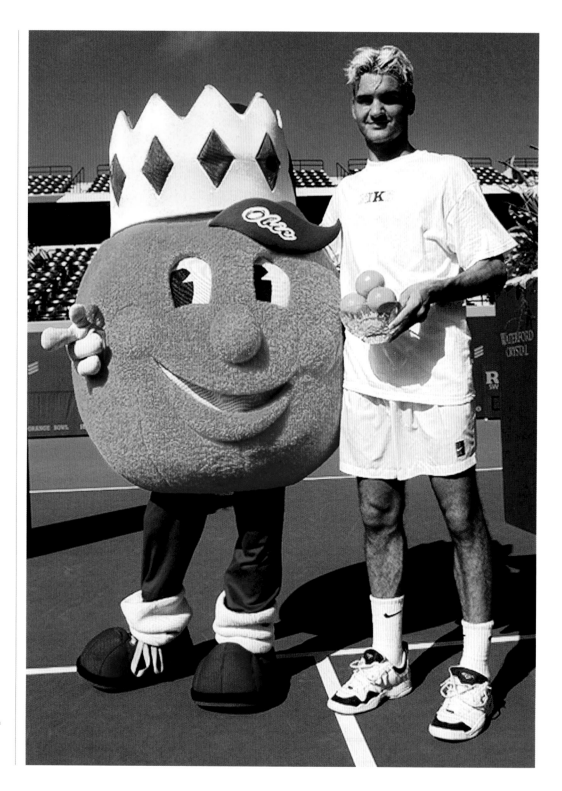

RIGHT: The teenager rounded off his magnificent 1998 season with a win at the Orange Bowl in Florida, beating Argentinian Guillermo Coria in the final.

Coria in the final. By the end of the year, he was the number one ranked junior in the world, just outside the Top 300 men.

Federer's senior ranking would improve to 64th by the end of 1999 – making him the youngest player in the Top 100 – but the year was more memorable for the teenager following his debuts in both the Davis Cup and the Grand Slams. The 17-year-old from Basel was beginning to circulate in the upper echelons of tennis and, although still a relative novice, it was obvious it would not be long before he was making serious inroads at the major tournaments.

His entry into the Davis Cup for Switzerland came in the World Group in April on the indoor carpet in Neuchâtel against Italy. Federer won his opening match against the experienced Davide Sanguinetti 6-4, 6-7, 6-3, 6-4 and although he was beaten second time out by Gianluca Pozzi, the priceless point he had already secured helped the Swiss win 3-2 and qualify for the quarter-finals.

The following month saw Federer play in his first-ever senior Grand Slam, as he headed to Paris to play at the Stade Roland Giros in the French Open. He lost in four sets in the first round to Australian Pat Rafter but his long-lasting affair with the majors had begun. In 1999, the tennis world had its first, tantalizing glimpse of the Swiss in the main draw at Wimbledon, a watershed moment which ended dramatically in the first round after an epic five-set reverse against Czech Jicí Novák.

Debuts in the Australian and US Opens followed in 2000, but the Swiss enhanced his reputation even further on the international stage by reaching the semi-finals of the men's singles at the Sydney Olympics. It was in Australia, and at the Games, that Federer first met Mirka Vavrinec, who was

LEFT: After debut appearances at in the main draw at Roland Garros and Wimbledon in 1999, the Swiss made his bow in the Australian and US Open the following season.

his place, Swede Peter Lundgren, an employee of the Swiss Tennis Federation, was drafted in and with his fresh perspective on the youngster's already impressive progress, the pair planned for 2001. Federer was up to 29th in the world and with such a lofty platform so early in the 19-year-old's career, the expectation was that he was now ready to make significant strides forward.

The year began with proof positive the teenager was undeniably the real deal with victory in Australia's Hopman Cup, partnering Martina Hingis, followed by his first ATP tour title in February at the Milan Indoor. After knocking out heavyweights Goran Ivanišević and Yevgeny Kafelnikov en route to the final, Federer joined an elite club of ATP champions with a 6-4, 7-6, 6-4 win over Frenchman Julien Boutter watched by his parents from the stands. Between 2001 and the end of 2018, the remarkable Swiss would appear in a staggering and record-breaking 150 ATP finals.

His moment of glory in Milan was merely a taste of what was to come. At the French Open, he reached the first Grand Slam quarter-final of his career and the following month he repeated the feat at Wimbledon. His headline-grabbing performance in SW19 in 2001, however, far surpassed anything he achieved in Paris.

At Wimbledon, Federer comfortably beat Olivier Rochus from Belgium in three sets in the first round. Another Belgian, Xavier Malisse, was sent home after a five-setter in the next round and Sweden's Jonas Björkman was his next victim as he marched into the last 16. Momentum was firmly with the fearless Federer but between him and a place in the quarter-finals stood Pete Sampras, the seven-time and defending Wimbledon champion, a then 12-time Grand Slam winner and a player who had been the dominant force in men's tennis for nearly a decade. The American, former world number one, had not been beaten on the SW19 grass for five years – a supreme sequence of 31 victories – and at the age of 29, was still at the peak of his sporting powers.

Many predicted that Federer would be little more than a sacrificial lamb in proceedings but

representing Switzerland in the women's singles and doubles. The pair became a couple in Sydney and nine years later were married in Riehen, near his home town of Basel.

The Olympic year also saw Federer end his working relationship with coach Peter Carter. In

rather than yield to the ferocity of Sampras's legendary serve and power game, the youngster stood firm and after three incredible hours and 41 minutes, it was the heir apparent who had emerged victorious over the king of Centre Court to signal a tectonic shift in the men's game.

The Swiss took the first set on a 9-7 tiebreak but Sampras rallied to clinch the second 7-5 with a single break of serve. It was 6-4 to Federer in the third before the reigning champion claimed the fourth on another tiebreak, and, to the delight of a packed Centre Court, the match went into the fifth. The decisive moment came when Federer broke Sampras's booming serve with the incredible athleticism and accuracy on return which he had displayed all day and he delivered the coup de grâce courtesy of a thunderous forehand down the line to win the set 7-5, and the match. The youngster failed to fight back the tears as it dawned on him the magnitude of his achievement while Sampras was left to contemplate his earliest Wimbledon exit in 10 years.

"You know, something great isn't going to last forever," the American said. "Today, I came up a little short. There are a lot of young guys coming up but Roger is a bit extra special. He has a great all-round game, like me doesn't get too emotional and you have to give him a great deal of credit. I have won a lot of close matches here - last year's final for one - and fortunately over the years I have managed to come up with the big shot but this time I came up short.

"Against Roger, I had my chances but did not convert them, whereas he played really well at the right time which is the key on grass. I plan on being back for many years. The reason I play tennis is to play in these big tournaments. There is no reason to panic and think I cannot come back and win here again."

The headline in The New York Times after the match read "Sampras, King of Wimbledon, is Dethroned" and, despite his optimism, "Pistol Pete" never triumphed in SW19 again. Federer had brought to an abrupt end the reign of the tournament's greatest ever champion to date.

"The Wimbledon clock stopped dead for Pete Sampras at 6.20 p.m. precisely yesterday," said

PREVIOUS PAGE: Yet to celebrate his 20th birthday, the Swiss headed to Wimbledon in 2001 hoping to progress past the first round at the All England Club for the first time.

OPPOSITE: An epic victory over Sampras on Centre Court, dethroning the seven-time SW19 winner, confirmed Federer's credentials as a future champion.

the *Guardian*. "After eight years of almost total dominance, the seven-times champion slowly, wearily gathered up his rackets, shirts, and towels, shouldered his black tennis bag, and walked slowly away a beaten man, having lost 7-6, 5-7, 6-4, 6-7, 7-5 in the fourth round to the 19-year-old Swiss Roger Federer, making his Centre Court debut, and never having won a match at the championships before last week.

"This was no fluke. Federer, the world junior number one three years ago, is widely recognized as one of the most gifted young players of his generation, and is already ranked number 15. But it was a quite extraordinary victory, Federer playing with the sort of sustained brilliance that Sampras displayed here in 1993 when he won the first of his Wimbledon titles."

It was something of an anticlimax when

"A lot of friends and players told me, 'This year, I think you can really beat him.' I'd played a great year so far, better than he had. I knew I had a chance. But it was not like 100 per cent. I mean, he's the man on grass. It feels unbelievable, of course. I knew it was not going to be easy. I'm very happy about my performance today, from the first to the last point. At times, I thought I was dreaming."

Federer *reflects on his 2001 Wimbledon victory over Pete Sampras*

OPPOSITE: Federer made his debut in the end-of-season ATP World Tour Finals in Shanghai in 2002, bowing out in the semi-finals to world number one Lleyton Hewitt.

Federer was vanquished by home favourite Tim Henman in the subsequent quarter-final but the teenager left London in buoyant mood. Even though the rest of his campaign was hampered by a thigh injury, costing him a debut in the prestigious end-of-season ATP Masters, he had the consolation of ending the year with a career-high ranking of 13th in the world.

Sadly, 2002 was a year of personal tragedy, as well frustrating highs and lows on the court. There were three ATP tour titles but he struggled to make a serious impression on Grand Slam duty, not least and most disappointingly at Wimbledon when he succumbed to a straight-sets, first-round loss to Croatia Mario Ancic. He nonetheless qualified for the Masters for the first time at the Shanghai New International Expo Centre in November and reached the semi-final stage before falling to eventual champion Lleyton Hewitt of Australia.

What unfolded on court in 2002, however, was largely overshadowed by news in early August of the sudden death of his former coach, mentor and friend Peter Carter after a car accident in South Africa. Federer was told of the premature demise of the 37-year-old during the Masters Series event in Toronto and it had a profound impact on the young man. The Swiss wore a black armband in memory of Carter in his next game – a third-round doubles match in Canada – but he was palpably struggling to come to terms with the news. "We spent a lot of time together since I was a boy," he said in an interview after the game. "I saw him every day growing up. It's terrible. He died so young and unexpectedly. Peter was very calm but he was also funny with a typical Australian sense of humour. I can never thank him enough for everything that he gave to me. Thanks to him I have my entire technique and coolness."

It would take Federer time to recover but regroup he did for 2003 and, despite the heartbreak over the loss of Carter, it was a year which saw him fulfil the incredible potential which his former coach had seen so clearly a decade earlier.

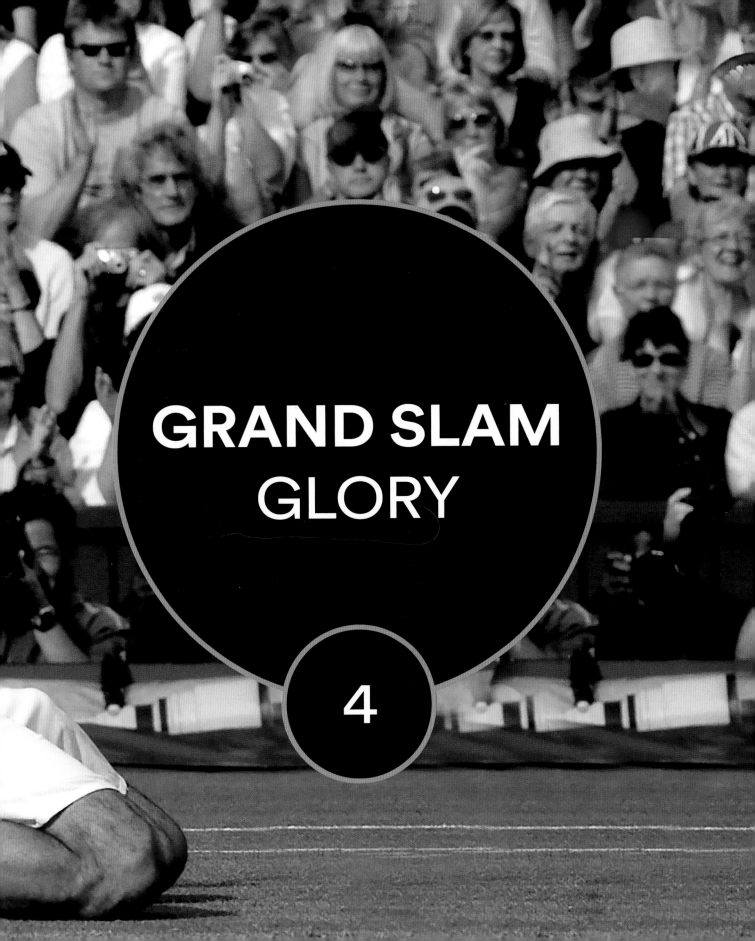

GRAND SLAM
GLORY

4

GRAND SLAM GLORY

No player has claimed more major men's singles titles than Federer and 2003 was the year that saw the Swiss star begin his unprecedented and inexorable charge towards sporting immortality.

Greatness in tennis is ultimately gauged by Grand Slam victories. ATP tour titles, ranking points, success in the Davis Cup and Olympic medals are all coveted by world-class competitors but to be truly considered one of the game's legendary players, a major triumph is obligatory. By the start of 2003, such career affirmation had so far eluded Federer and, although he had risen to sixth in the world by the age of just 21, he had yet to progress past the quarter-finals in any of the four Slams.

The year began with a respectable, albeit disappointing fourth-round performance at the Australian Open and the French Open was once again an unhappy hunting ground, with Federer falling at the first hurdle. The grass season now appeared his best hope of making his major breakthrough and, having won at the Halle Open in Germany in early June, he headed to SW19 with renewed optimism.

His initial progress was serene enough but he suffered a back injury in his fourth-round victory over Feliciano López to cast a shadow over his chances. He recovered sufficiently to beat Holland's Sjeng Schalken and then fifth-seed American Andy Roddick to make it through to the final. For the first time in his career, he would play in the climax of a Grand Slam. His opponent on Centre Court was to be six-foot-five Australian Mark Philippoussis, a player with

one of the biggest and most destructive serves in tennis.

When it mattered most, the Swiss produced a near faultless display. He returned Philippoussis's booming serve with athletic aplomb while sending down some howitzers of his own and the Australian had no answer to his opponent's movement and superior ground strokes. Federer ran out a 7-6, 6-2, 7-6 winner and after the final point, the Centre Court crowd rose to salute its new champion.

"He may not be the 17–year–old symbol of a nation, as Boris Becker was when he won the title," wrote Christopher Clarey in the *New York Times*. "He may not exude the Nordic mystery of Björn Borg or have the Big Apple mouth of John McEnroe. But there is something magnetic about Federer's tennis, an attractive blend of smooth moving and creative thinking, of tact and force that has the potential to cut across borders."

Federer's performance left a lasting impression on all those who witnessed his triumph, not least the BBC tennis correspondent Jonathan Overend. "There was one shot from the final I remember as if it were yesterday," he wrote. "It was a half-volley around the service line, and he skipped into it from the baseline in that very fluid way that Federer has. You would have expected him to play with soft hands, maybe look for the drop shot, but

PREVIOUS PAGE: The greatest male player in the history of Wimbledon, Federer's love affair with the oldest of the four Grand Slams has endured for two decades.

LEFT: Federer was unable to contain himself after beating Australian Mark Philippoussis on Centre Court in the 2003 Wimbledon final to claim the first Grand Slam title of his era-defining career.

instead he drove through it with so much topspin. By rights, it should have hit the backboard on the full, but somehow he managed to get it up and down for a winner. I don't think I've seen another shot like that, before or since."

The win confirmed that the Swiss had genuinely arrived and he finished the year in style, winning the Masters in Houston for the first time after beating Andre Agassi. He ended the season in the lofty position of two in the world and set his sights on underlining his status as the circuit's new man to beat.

His first assignment of 2004 saw him at the Australian Open. Many pundits were convinced Federer had the natural game to prosper down under and they were proved right as he cruised into a debut semi-final at Melbourne Park. His convincing 6-4, 6-1, 6-4 win over Juan Carlos Ferrero of Spain in the last four merely strengthened the belief the Swiss's time in Australia had come.

The victory was significant for two reasons. Firstly, it propelled him into his first Melbourne final but it also confirmed Federer would be the new world number one when the updated rankings were released. He would hold the top spot for an incredible 237 consecutive weeks through to August 2008, and in the history of the ATP rankings, introduced in 1974, no player before or since has even come close to matching that record-breaking feat.

Federer faced Marat Safin in the final. The Russian had deposed of top-seed Roddick in the quarters and defending champion Agassi in the last four. The ensuing showpiece game was, in truth, more of a procession rather than a thriller as the Swiss dominated from start to finish, and after two hours and 15 minutes on the Rod Laver Court, he had beaten Safin 7-6, 6-4, 6-2. Federer was the Australian Open champion for the first time and now a two-time Grand Slam champion.

"To win the Australian Open and become number one in the world is a dream come true," Federer said. "I feel as if I'm living the game when I'm out there. I feel when a guy is going to hit the ball I know exactly the angles and the spins. And that's a huge advantage. It's also important that I can always feel I can raise my game."

John Parsons in the *Telegraph* wrote: "Federer is now acknowledged as having the most complete game in tennis. When Federer did step up the pace and put away those devastating forehands, it was

OPPOSITE: The 23-year-old Swiss began 2004 with a second Grand Slam triumph after he beat Marat Safin in Melbourne in the climax of the Australian Open.

enough to underpin his status on top of the world rankings and convince John McEnroe that he is good enough to become the first man to win all four Slams in the same year since Rod Laver in 1969."

At Wimbledon, in the summer, the Swiss was once again in imperious form and marched back into the final for the loss of just two sets. The familiar face of Roddick was on the opposite side of the net on Centre Court and the second seed took early control of proceedings, taking the first set 6-4 and going a break up in the second. The defending champion was on the ropes in what was a rain-

LEFT: Federer returned to
the All England Club in 2004
to successfully defend his
crown, beating American Andy
Roddick in four sets in the final.

affected contest but after the second stoppage caused by inclement weather, he rediscovered his rhythm. After saving six break points in the fourth set, Federer held his nerve to complete a 4-6, 7-5, 7-6, 6-4 triumph. He confirmed the successful defence of his title with an ace and, as he had done 12 months earlier, Federer sank to his knees in tears after wrapping up a second Wimbledon title. Victory marked the beginning of Federer's record sequence of reaching 23 consecutive Grand Slam semi-finals and 36 consecutive quarter-finals, in which he reached 19 finals and won 14 Slams.

Next up on the radar was the US Open and it surprised no one when Federer continued his rich vein of form by reaching the final for the first time, albeit after a five-set epic against Agassi in the quarter-final. He faced Lleyton Hewitt at Flushing Meadows and the form book suggested a tight encounter. The Australian reached the final without dropping a set, was on a 16-match winning streak and boasted an eight-five winning career record against the Swiss, while Federer had beaten him at both Melbourne and Wimbledon earlier in the season.

Statistics, however, can be misleading and so it proved in the final as Federer spectacularly demolished his man in New York. The first set lasted a mere 18 minutes as the Swiss took it 6-0 and although Hewitt rallied enough to take the second to a tiebreak, he lost it, while the third was all one-way traffic as Federer once again took all six games without reply. He had now added the US Open title to his burgeoning collection.

"Not until he was 6-0, 2-0 down did Hewitt, who like Federer is 23, finally get his name on the scoreboard," wrote Stephen Bierley in The Guardian. "It was not that he was playing badly, simply that Federer's form was awesome. Hewitt, like Tim Henman [in the semi-final] had tried his best, but Federer is currently a class apart from everyone."

His demolition job meant Federer became only the 10th player to win three Grand Slam titles in a calendar year and the first to achieve the season hat-trick since the revered Swede Mats Wilander 16 years earlier. Victory also saw the Swiss become

LEFT: The Swiss arrived at Flushing Meadows for the 2004 US Open aiming to seal his third Grand Slam of the year and his first triumph in New York.

the first man in the history of the game to triumph in his first four major finals.

The 23-year-old signed off in 2004 with yet more silverware when he successfully defended his Masters title in Houston, once again shattering the hopes of Hewitt in the final. His win made yet more history – no player in the Open Era had ever won three Grand Slam titles and the year-end championship in the same year. In the 12 months, Federer claimed 11 singles titles, which was the most for any male player in two decades and his overall record of 74 singles wins and just six defeats was the most prolific since Ivan Lendl in 1986.

The world of tennis waited expectantly in 2005 to see how Federer could possibly follow such a remarkable season of dominance but before he took to the court, there was news of a new coach with the appointment of Tony Roche. The Swiss had been without a full-time coach since he had parted company with Peter Lundgren in 2003 and he hoped the arrival of Australian Roche, the 1966 French Open champion and four-time Grand Slam finalist, would help to improve his performances on clay, the only surface he had yet to truly master.

Federer surrendered his Australian Open crown early in the year – losing to Marat Safin in a five-set, semi-final marathon – but any fears he might struggle to replicate the pyrotechnics of 2004 were allayed in the next three majors. The French Open did not yield the Roland-Garros title he craved but he reached the semi-final for the first time in Paris, losing to eventual champion Rafael Nadal, only the third time the two great rivals had crossed swords in their careers and their first encounter on clay.

At Wimbledon, however, it was back to business as usual. Only Germany's Nicolas Kiefer was able to take a set from the reigning champion as he cruised into the final and there was an overwhelming sense of déjà vu when it emerged he would face Roddick in the final, a repeat of their 2004 showdown. The American had already lost eight of their previous nine meetings and had good reason to be sick of the sight of his opponent after losing the final again, going down 6-2, 7-6,

6-4 well inside two hours. The champion blasted down 15 winners in a one-sided opening set alone and there was already no way back for Hewitt.

A third consecutive Wimbledon title was sweet enough but his triumph also made the 23-year-old only the third player after the legendary Pete Sampras and Björn Borg to win a major for three consecutive years in the Open Era.

"I couldn't have asked for more or wanted it more but this guy's the best for a reason and deserves credit," Roddick conceded. "He's become such a complete player, even since he beat me in the semi-finals two years ago. He's improved so much since then. He's probably as close as there's been to unbeatable. I felt like I played decent, the stats were decent and I got beat in straight sets. You're not stretching far to make the argument he's the best ever. I don't know many people in history who could beat him."

The Swiss's defence of his US Open title in August was almost as convincing as he had been in SW19. None of his opponents realistically threatened to derail his progress at Flushing Meadows and it was home-favourite Agassi who would provide the opposition in the final. At 35, the Las Vegan was the oldest Grand Slam finalist since Ken Rosewall in 1974 (a record Federer himself would subsequently break in 2018) but with eight majors on his CV, including the elusive career Grand Slam, he had the pedigree to ask questions of the world number one.

Those questions were particularly pertinent after Agassi took the second set 6-2 after Federer had claimed the first 6-3. The American was also a break up in the third but the champion was able to extinguish the threat quickly to win the subsequent tiebreak before running away with it 6-1 in the fourth and final set. Victory gave Federer a sixth major title, drawing him level on the all-time list with his childhood hero Boris Becker and Stefan Edberg.

"I think Roger is the best I've played against," said Agassi after losing what was to be the last major final appearance of his own glittering career. "To watch him evolve has been amazing. There's nowhere to go. With other guys, there is a safety zone. Against Roger, anything you try to do, he has the answer. He plays the game in a very special way that I haven't seen before. And he does it over and over again.

"There are periods in a match when you can have him against the fence, but his options are better than anybody else. He can hurt you at any point. The pressure you feel against him is different to anyone else and does things the others just can't do. Roger makes you play on the edge. You need to play the craziest tennis you've ever played."

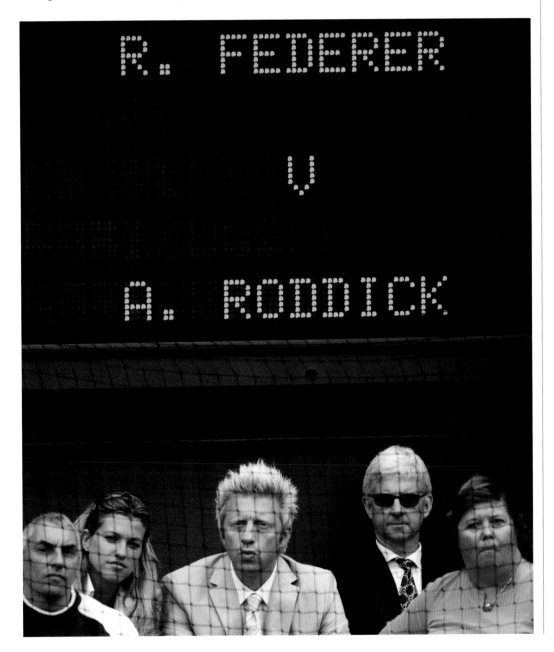

R. FEDERER

V

A. RODDICK

LEFT: Federer's childhood hero Boris Becker was at Centre Court in 2005 to witness the Swiss claim his third Wimbledon title after victory over Roddick.

"I proved it to everybody and it was a big relief because there was pressure from all sides, especially from myself, to do better in Slams. I knew I had the game and I have always believed in myself. I kept my level up here in the semi-finals and the final, and to lift the trophy is an absolute dream. You need a little luck like I had with my back when I struggled through that match. I was in big pain – I was struggling to serve, to return, even to sit down. Somehow I stayed in but at that point I didn't think I would ever hold the trophy."

Federer *on winning his first Wimbledon crown.*

OPPOSITE: The final of the 2005 US Open was a battle of the generations as the 24-year-old Swiss overcame the veteran Andre Agassi at Flushing Meadows.

A SPORTING
PHENOMENON

5

A **SPORTING** PHENOMENON

The winner of six Grand Slam titles by the age of 24, the Swiss sensation continued to rewrite the tennis record books between 2006 and 2008 as he irresistibly tightened his grip on the men's game with seven more major triumphs.

Complacency is not a characteristic associated with elite athletes. The burning desire to push the boundaries of what is possible is a common trait among serial champions and so it was with Federer as he prepared for his assault on the 2006 season and yet more silverware. Two major triumphs the previous year was an imperious effort but the Swiss, as ever, wanted more. The latter stages of his 2005 campaign had been curtailed by a foot injury – which in part explained his shock defeat to David Nalbandian in the end-of-season Masters in China – but he returned in the new year restored to full fitness and eager to remind his rivals that he was still the undisputed king of the court.

His mission began as ever in Melbourne at the Australian Open in January. The lower-ranked challengers of the early rounds were duly dispatched with elegance and little alarm and, although he dropped a set to both Tommy Haas and Nikolay Davydenko en route, he cruised into the final to face the unseeded 20-year-old Cypriot Marco Baghdatis.

No one believed the unheralded youngster had the weaponry to trouble Federer but the challenger refused to follow the script and stunned the crowd inside the Rod Laver Arena by taking the first set 7-5. In game three of the second set, the Cypriot had points for a double break but the Swiss decided enough was enough,

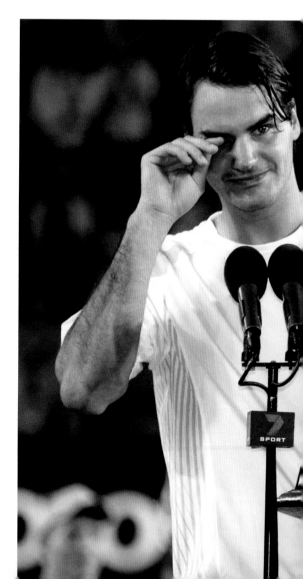

PREVIOUS PAGE: Federer's triumph at Wimbledon in 2006 was the second instalment of a Grand Slam hat-trick in another dominant campaign for the world number one.

steadied the ship and subsequently rattled off 11 consecutive games to seal a four-set victory.

The new champion received his trophy from Laver himself, on the court named in honour of the 11-time Grand Slam winner, and the moment was made yet more emotional by the presence of the family of the late Peter Carter, Federer's coach and friend who had died suddenly nearly four years earlier. As the reigning Wimbledon, US and now Australian champion, Federer became the first player since Pete Sampras to win three majors on the bounce.

A second final came in June in Paris as he reached the showpiece match of the French Open for the first time in his career. But it was Rafael Nadal, his nemesis on clay and the defending champion, who stood ominously in his way. Against the majority of the pre-match predictions, Federer convincingly took the opening set 6-1 but was unable to halt the Spaniard's ferocious comeback and, in the end, succumbed to a 6-1, 1-6, 4-6, 6-7 defeat. His dream of completing the fabled career Grand Slam was over for another year.

"I really want to congratulate Rafael," he said. "He is so strong on clay and played a really good match. He is so hard to beat on this surface. He's performed a great season on clay and during the fortnight. He truly deserves to win. Obviously, it's a pity but I tried."

LEFT: An emotional Federer claimed his second Australian Open title and seventh Major in early 2006, receiving the trophy from the legendary Rod Laver in Melbourne.

Solace, not to mention revenge, was soon on hand, however, with the start of his beloved Wimbledon and the champion was faultless on the grass as he glided effortlessly into yet another final without the loss of a single set. Nadal, appearing in his first final in SW19, was the man charged with stopping him but the game was something of a mirror image of their encounter in Paris weeks earlier. This time, however, the surface was Federer's and although the young Spaniard did take a set, he was ultimately outgunned and condemned to a 6-0, 7-6, 6-7, 6-4 defeat.

Victory gave the Swiss his fourth SW19 crown – only the seventh man ever to achieve a quartet of trophies. "Federer is starting to remind me of Borg," wrote two-time Wimbledon champion Jimmy Connors on the BBC website after the match. "Not just in the way he's dominating Wimbledon year after year, but also in his approach to the sport. In my playing days, I could never get to Borg, never knew what he was thinking. Federer is just the same, especially in his attitude and the way he never lets himself gets flustered. Federer has already taken his place in history."

The long flight across the Atlantic to play in the US Open the following month did little to diminish his powers and for the third time in his career, Federer faced Andy Roddick in a major final. The American fared little better at Flushing Meadows than he had on the two previous occasions at Wimbledon as the Swiss registered a four-set victory, in the process sending the game's statisticians scrambling to update their record books once again.

Federer was the first man since the great Rod Laver in 1969 to reach all four Grand Slam finals in the same year. His ninth major moved him into sixth place in the game's all-time list while his New York triumph meant the Swiss had recorded three successive wins in both the US Open and Wimbledon, a first in tennis history.

There was still enough time in 2006 for him to record two more significant entries on his CV. In October, he won the Swiss Indoors in Basel for the first time, eight years after his debut in the

home town tournament where he had once been a ballboy, while in November he regained his Masters crown in Shanghai. His 2006 campaign was statistically the best of Federer's incredible career and second only to Laver's fabled Grand Slam year in 1969. He won 92 of his 97 singles matches en route to his 12 titles – the most since John McEnroe 22 years earlier – and, perhaps most incredibly, he reached the finals of 16 of the 17 ATP events in which he played.

ABOVE: Federer's win over Andy Roddick in the 2006 US Open final elevated him to sixth on the all-time list of Grand Slam champions with nine Major titles.

OPPOSITE: Federer poses with his Wimbledon trophy and girlfriend Mirka Vavrinec at the Wimbledon Winners' Dinner at the Savoy Hotel on July 9, 2006.

The records continued to tumble with unerring regularity in 2007. There was only one show in town in Melbourne for the Australian Open and after the Swiss had disposed of Fernando González 7-6, 6-4, 6-4 in the final, he became the first player since Borg in 1980 to claim a major without a dropping a single set. The following month, he went past Connors' long-standing record of 160 successive weeks at the pinnacle of the ATP world rankings.

His summer sojourn in Paris, however, proved distinctly unsatisfactory as he fell at the final hurdle again in the French Open against Nadal. Federer had beaten the Spaniard for the first time on clay in Hamburg only a few weeks earlier, ending Nadal's 81-match-winning run on the surface, but on the bigger stage of Roland-Garros, he came up short. The two great rivals shared the first two sets but Nadal edged the third and fourth to replicate his 3-1 victory on the Court Philippe-Chatrier of 12 months earlier.

If events in Paris were frustratingly familiar, the remainder of the year offered its now-customary sense of redemption as the Swiss swept all before him in England and then the US. Wimbledon was his opportunity to equal the Open Era record of five consecutive titles at the All England Club and his seemingly effortless progression through the rounds to the final suggested the reigning champion was a safe bet to register the quintet. In the other half of the draw, however, Nadal was also building up a head of steam but when it was confirmed the final would be a repeat of their 2006 clash, most believed Federer would again prevail in what had become his own backyard.

The match that actually unfolded enthralled the Centre Court crowd for three thrilling hours and 45 minutes. A tense first set went in favour of the champion on a tiebreak, only for the challenger to level up the scores after taking the second set 6-4. Another tiebreak edged by the Swiss made it 2-1 but Nadal broke twice in the fourth to take the final

ABOVE: A three-set victory over Chile's Fernando González in the final of the Australian Open saw Federer start the 2007 season in characteristically imposing form.

decisive fifth set. It was the first time Federer had ever gone all the way in a Slam final and when he faced four break points in the sixth game, it looked as though it may be a bridge too far for the older of the two men. A trademark forehand drive down the line got him out of jail and Nadal seemed to visibly wilt and the champion closed out in commanding style, winning the fifth 6-2 to conclude one of the greatest finals in Wimbledon history.

"In a matter of moments, three sides of Roger Federer were on display at Centre Court," said the *New York Times*. "First came the deft and forceful overhead smash that won him the Wimbledon championship. Then came the emotional reaction: Federer dropped to his knees, rolled on to his back with his hands over his face, and sat up with tears in his eyes.

"Finally, to the rousing cheers of fans, including Björn Borg, Federer came gliding in to accept the winner's trophy. He wore a sheepish grin and — after a Superman-like change of clothes — his trademark white trousers, white vest and white monogrammed blazer with gold trim. There is always a dash of style with Federer and now he has reached a nearly unprecedented level of substance."

BELOW: A repeat of the 2006 final, the climax of the 2007 men's singles at Wimbledon saw the champion once again overcome the challenge of Nadal.

His five wins on the bounce equalled Borg's record and also took him to 11 majors, level with the great Swede and Laver in third on the all-time Grand Slam victory list. Only Australian Roy Emerson, who won 12 in the 1960s, and Sampras with 14 now stood above him.

"Each one is special but to play a champion like Rafa, it means a lot and equalling Björn's record as well," Federer admitted. "It was such a close match. I told him at the net that he deserved it as well. I'm the lucky one today."

It was always going to be a tall order to replicate such pure drama at the subsequent US Open and, in truth, although Federer went on to to clinch his fourth successive title at Flushing Meadows, it was a far more prosaic triumph. The world number one dropped just two sets throughout the tournament and came up against third-seed Novak Djokovic, dispatching the then up-and-coming Serbian in straight sets, albeit with the first two going to a tiebreak.

The season ended with Federer clinching a fourth Masters title and as 2007 ebbed away, he was the year-end world number one for a fourth consecutive campaign. Statistically, he was tantalizingly short of his 2006 heroics but had, nonetheless, reached all four Grand Slam finals and only strengthened the opinion of many seasoned tennis observers that he was already the greatest ever player to pick up a racket.

The Federer story so far had been on a relentless, upward trajectory but 2008 – a decade after making his professional debut on the ATP tour – was the year in which, by his own stratospheric standards, he struggled. There was the considerable consolation of an Olympic gold medal and another US Open success but there were also more lows than he had previously experienced in his breathless rise to the top of the sport.

He was dethroned as the Australian Open champion by Djokovic in the semi-finals in Melbourne, unceremoniously ending his incredible sequence of 10 consecutive Grand Slam finals, while in early March he revealed he had been suffering from glandular fever since December.

OPPOSITE: A fifth straight Wimbledon title arrived as Federer once again downed his great rival Rafael Nadal. The elation – and relief – was clear to see.

OPPOSITE: Federer's straight sets win over Novak Djokovic in the 2007 US Open final was the first time the two rivals had met in the denouement of a Grand Slam tournament.

ABOVE: After near misses at the
French Open and Wimbledon,
Federer returned to winning
ways in 2008 at the US Open
with victory in the final against
Andy Murray.

A third successive defeat to Nadal in the final of the French Open – this time a comprehensive and chastening 1-6, 3-6, 0-6 defeat – did nothing to improve his confidence. Despite this, he headed to Wimbledon in the hope that playing at his spiritual home would revive his fortunes.

All seemed well as the Swiss progressed to the final without the loss of a set. Centre Court was set to stage the latest instalment of his rivalry with Nadal after the Spaniard reached the final in similarly commanding style. What happened next would live long in the memory of every tennis fan

sixth, successive All England Club crown. The rain-affected match, however, had plenty more to give and when the Swiss began his fightback, taking the third 7-6, with a 7-5 win in the tiebreak, the crowd sensed a turn in the tide. The fourth set also went to a tiebreak and when the reigning champion edged it 10-8, dramatically saving two match points in the process, the second with an outrageous backhand winner, it was time for the protagonists to settle matters with a fifth and final set. Neither was able to break the other in the first 14 games but in the 15th, Nadal pounced to edge ahead and then served out for a 9-7 scoreline and his maiden SW19 title.

Defeat in what, at four hours and 48 minutes, was the longest Wimbledon final in history was heartbreaking. Federer was left to rue his failure to convert only one of his 13 break points in the match and after 65 consecutive victories on grass, he was no longer the champion. "Federer suffered the unpleasant experience of watching, dejected, from his chair as he came to terms with finishing runner-up for the first time," reported the BBC. "It may be little consolation but he played his part in one of the great finals."

Federer had precious-little time to regroup from the seismic shock of losing on Centre Court as the US Open was just around the corner. Perhaps surprisingly, he looked in good spirits at Flushing Meadows, despite having surrendered his number one ranking to Nadal after his record-breaking, 237-week reign at the top. He knew the only way to address his recent setbacks was on court and although he was taken to five sets in the fourth round by the Russian Igor Andreev, his march to the final was very much vintage Federer, as was his performance in the final against Britain's Andy Murray. A 6-2, 7-5, 6-2 triumph gave him a 13th Grand Slam title and a timely fillip after what he acknowledged had been a difficult year.

"It definitely feels great," he said. "This is a very special moment in my career. I had a couple of tough Grand Slams this year, so to take this one home is incredible. It means the world to me. I'm not going to stop at 13."

and is now widely considered the greatest match of all time.

The challenger drew first blood in the opening set, taking it 6-4, and when he clinched the second by the same scoreline, it appeared he was on course to halt Federer's bid for a historic

"Roger has so much talent but the main thing is that he so enjoys playing the game. It's easy to get mentally drained and for the desire to ebb if you have to grind out matches, but Roger loves playing. And when things are not working, he tries something else and finds a way to win. His court coverage and his anticipation are uncanny and if his backhand is in shape, he just seems to roll."

Rod Laver *on Federer after his victory in the 2006 Australian Open*

OPPOSITE: His three-set triumph over Murray in the Arthur Ashe Stadium gave the Swiss the 13th Major of his career, leaving Federer just one Grand Slam title behind Pete Sampras.

OLYMPIC SUCCESS

6

OLYMPIC SUCCESS

A four-time Olympian, Federer first competed at the Games in Sydney in 2000. Eight years later, he stood on the podium in Beijing, the Swiss national anthem playing as he proudly held the coveted Olympic gold medal.

Few athletes are privileged enough to experience the unique atmosphere of an Olympics during their career. They are the pinnacle of almost every sport and since the inaugural modern Games in Athens in 1896, tennis's finest have vied with each other for the right to call themselves an Olympic champion. Many have tried but only a select few have ever achieved the feat. Roger Federer became a member of the exclusive club in China in 2008 when he and Stanislas Wawrinka triumphed in the men's doubles event. Their success made them national heroes back home in Switzerland and, by his own admission, victory in Beijing remains one of the highlights of Federer's already glittering career.

The first chapter of his Olympic story, however, was written in 2000 when the 19-year-old was selected to represent Switzerland in Sydney. The teenager was ranked number 36 in the world when he headed down under for the men's singles event. As a result, he was not one of the 16 seeds in the competition, and he travelled more in hope than expectation of emulating the heroics of compatriot Marc Rosset, who had won gold for Switzerland eight years earlier.

The youngster, nonetheless, breezed through the early rounds in Sydney and after he had put away Karim Alami from Morocco 7-6, 6-1 in the quarter-final, he was unexpectedly within touching distance of a medal. Defeat to Germany's Tommy Haas in the last four was a body blow but a bronze medal was still a possibility if he could overcome Frenchman Arnaud Di Pasquale in a play-off. The first two sets were both settled by tiebreaks, resulting in a 1-1 scoreline, but it was Di Pasquale who held his nerve in the decider to take

it 6-3 and deny his opponent any tangible reward for his efforts. "Considering how the match was going, I should never have lost," Federer said, fighting back the tears. "I really wanted to be standing on the podium. Now I have nothing to take home except my pride."

It was an altogether more mature, feared and famous Swiss player who returned to the Olympics in Athens in 2004. Fresh from wins at the Australian Open and Wimbledon earlier in the year, he was the best player in the world according to the ATP and had a global profile. As a result, the National Olympic Committee for Switzerland bestowed on him the honour of carrying the national flag at the opening ceremony. Leading out the Swiss team in front of a worldwide audience in

the billions was, sadly, to prove the highlight of his Games.

The top seed made it safely out of the first round of the men's singles when he beat Russian Nikolay Vladimirovich in three sets but he was surprisingly dumped out of the tournament next time out, losing 6-4, 5-7, 5-7 to the unseeded Czech Tomáš Berdych, the world number 74. It was a frustratingly similar story in the men's doubles. Federer was paired with Yves Allegro, his old friend from their junior days in Switzerland, but the duo's well-established dynamic was not enough to prevent a second-round exit at the hands of India's Mahesh Bhupathi and Leander Paes.

Federer returned for a third attempt at claiming an elusive Olympic medal in Beijing in 2008. He was technically still number one in the world rankings, although top spot would be officially conferred to Rafael Nadal the day after tennis at the Games had concluded, ending his four-and-a-half year-reign. On the same day that he celebrated his 27th birthday, he once again was at the front of Team Switzerland for the pyrotechnics of the opening ceremony.

"It is a true honour for me to lead the Swiss athletes into the stadium, carrying the Swiss flag," he said. "I have had the privilege to experience many wonderful things and the Olympics are and will always be one of the best. So I am really looking forward to those moments. This is one of the most wonderful birthday presents I could possibly wish for. It's well known that I still have a score to settle with the Olympics and being handed this honour for a second time will give me extra motivation."

His quest for redemption began in the men's singles and a first-round clash with Dmitry Tursunov. The Russian offered little significant resistance at the Olympic Green Tennis Centre in a 6-4, 6-2 victory for the Swiss. When Federer then beat El Salvadorian Rafael Arévalo González in straight sets in round two, he had already progressed further than he had in Greece four years earlier. A familiar foe stood in his path in round three in the shape of Berdych, his Athens conqueror, but this time the top seed made no

mistake against his lower-ranked opponent and exacted his revenge with a 6-3, 7-6 win.

Unseeded American James Blake lay in wait in the quarter-finals. Blake had failed to beat Federer in eight previous meetings but had never played a match in which the Swiss made so many unforced errors and took the first set 6-4. The second went to a tiebreak but rather than level the scoreline, as the crowd expected, Federer faded and Blake took it 7-2 to send his illustrious opponent crashing out of the men's singles. "It's a big disappointment, obviously," Federer conceded. "The Olympics was one of the goals of the season for me. So the quarter-finals is not going to do it. I think James played well. I can only really say how well he played. I've played him on many occasions, but I think this was the best I've seen him. I'm happy for him. I hope he can go all the way now."

His Olympic challenge, however, was not yet over. Federer and Wawrinka, the world number 10, had already made it safely through the first two rounds of the men's doubles and the day after his shock fall to Blake, he was back on court in the quarter-finals to face the Indian duo of Bhupathi and Paes, the pairing who vanquished him and Allegro in 2004. This time, Switzerland were in the ascendency and reached the last four courtesy of a comfortable 6-2, 6-4 victory. It was a family affair later the same day in the semi-finals when the Swiss came up against the American Bryan brothers Bob and Mike, the top seeds in the tournament and previous winners of all four Grand Slam doubles titles. The first set was settled by a tense 8-6 tiebreak in favour of Federer and Wawrinka and when they broke Mike Bryan's serve in the seventh game of the second set, the Swiss pairing calmly served out 6-4 to reach the final that Federer so desperately craved.

After two games in a day, Federer and Wawrinka had less than 24 hours to recover before the gold medal match against the Swedish pairing of Simon Aspelin and Thomas Johansson, the 2002 Australian Open champion. As befitted a final, the contest was scheduled as a potential five-set affair rather than the abridged three sets of the earlier rounds. The Swiss began strongly, taking the

OPPOSITE: The Swiss was given the honour of carrying the Swiss flag at the National Stadium during the spectacular opening ceremony of the 2008 Beijing Olympics.

first set 6-3 and another single break was enough to give them the second 6-4. Federer's expansive shots were backed up by some inspired tennis from Wawrinka but the Swedes rallied and forced the third set to a tiebreak, taking the honours 7-4. The fourth set saw the Swiss break once again and it came down to Federer to serve out for the title, which he did with typically nerveless aplomb. The victorious teammates had won one of only two gold medals for Switzerland in Beijing and they celebrated their triumph wildly, crashing to the floor and embracing each other.

"Switzerland's Roger Federer could not stop hugging partner Stanislas Wawrinka after they beat Swedes Simon Aspelin and Thomas Johansson 6-3, 6-4, 6-7, 6-3 to win the Olympic men's doubles final on Saturday," reported Reuters. "The best player in the world for the past five years produced flashes of brilliance throughout the contest but he also owed much to his lesser-known opponent who played a full part in the Centre Court finale. Federer, who carried the Swiss flag at the opening ceremony, was clearly fired up throughout the contest.

"The 27-year-old, 12-times Grand Slam champion is usually cool and calm on court but on Saturday he was clenching his fists at crucial points and roaring praise at Wawrinka. He was clearly in no mood to let his chance slip this time. Fittingly, it was he who had the job of serving for gold at 5-3 in the fourth set. He duly obliged before embarking on a lap of honour with the Swiss flag."

Federer had finally realized his dream of Olympic glory. "This is quite a surreal moment," he admitted. "It's a joy sharing this victory with somebody else who I like very much, who we had a great two weeks with. We had played so well from the beginning to the end. We did it and I am unbelievably happy. The thing is, I can't just hug a stranger when I win singles. In singles you're all alone on the court. You win, you sit down."

Mission accomplished, the 27-year-old returned home to a hero's welcome in his home town of Basel and then to the ATP tour and his hunt for yet more majors. But the pull of the Olympics proved too strong four years later and Federer found himself in London – and the All England Club – to

"I'm thrilled, it's a big moment. It's a dream-come-true moment. It comes around maybe once in a lifetime. The feeling is almost disbelief, to some degree. It's not the first time this tournament or in my life I had to serve for a big match. It's basically the moment you dream of being in, even though there is so much pressure to it. This is the biggest sporting event in the world and you feel special to be in something so important. It's a magical moment, something incredible in my career."

Federer *on winning Olympic gold in Beijing in 2008*

OPPOSITE: A famous four-set victory in the final at the National Tennis Centre in Beijing gave Federer the first Olympic medal of his career.

compete in his fourth Games. "This is a once in a lifetime opportunity to be playing at Wimbledon at the Olympic Games," he said. "It's just a really big deal for us to be living that Olympic spirit, right there, at the most incredible arena we have in tennis. I don't think there's another player in singles who has played four [Olympic Games] in this era so I am very happy that I'm able to do this."

Before a ball was struck in London, however, there was the question of which athlete would lead out Team Switzerland at the Olympic Stadium at the opening of the 2012 Games. Federer was the obvious choice again but he declined to reprise his role as flag bearer and, as a result, it was Wawrinka who was chosen.

"I felt like maybe I could enter the history books by doing it a third time," he said. "It would have been amazing and there's no denying that I would have loved to do it. I just felt it was important to give someone else a chance. We do believe other people should also have chances. That's why I told Swiss Olympic [officials] I think they should choose someone else. I think it's a great, great honour for Stan. I could not have won Olympic gold without him."

For the first time in his Olympic career, Federer successfully fought his way through to the final of the men's singles in SW19 but a second gold medal ultimately escaped him. He was twice taken to three sets en route to the gold medal match, only to recover, but the Swiss had no answer in the final to Britain's Andy Murray, who thrived on the support of his vocal home crowd and powered his way to a 6-2, 6-1, 6-4 victory. Federer had to settle for adding silver to his Olympic collection and there was further disappointment in the doubles when he and Wawrinka surrendered their crown in the second round against the Israeli duo of Andy Ram and Yoni Erlich.

Remarkably, Federer was set to appear at his fifth Olympics in Rio de Janeiro in 2016 but was denied the chance to compete again by a season-ending knee injury, pulling out just two weeks before the start of the Games in Brazil. It was a cruel blow but one which did not end his Olympic love affair. "Wish I was there with you," he

tweeted from home in Switzerland as he watched the opening ceremony on television.

The Swiss will be 38-years-old by the time the Tokyo Olympics begin in July 2020. Even the seemingly ageless Federer will have to retire one

day but he has so far refused to rule out one last Olympic adventure, 22 years after he first wore the red and white of Switzerland in Sydney. "If I'm still playing, great," he said, "but I'm not saying I definitely have to play one more [Olympics] before I retire. If it happens, then it makes sense for me to go play, but it's too far away. I don't know. When the time is right, I'll talk about it – and see how I feel in that year. It would be nice. But I can't tell you for sure, or not for sure."

ABOVE: The Swiss' fourth appearance at the Games saw him beat Juan Martin Del Potro of Argentina on Centre Court to reach the final of the men's singles.

RIGHT: Federer faced home favourite Andy Murray in the final at the All England Club but had to settle for silver after succumbing to a three-set defeat.

THE CAREER
CLEAN SWEEP

7

CAREER CLEAN SWEEP

Fresh from his Olympic triumph in Beijing, Federer embarked on the 2009 season, the 12th of his professional career. It turned out to be a remarkable year, marking Federer as the most successful player ever to have graced the men's singles game.

By the age of 27, the Swiss had already achieved more in tennis than mere mortals dare dream of. With his prolific haul of 13 Grand Slam titles, five Masters crowns and an Olympic gold medal, as well as having spent more consecutive weeks as world number one than any other player, his raft of achievements was nothing short of stellar. Had he never stepped on to a court again, Federer could still have retired as, arguably, the greatest tennis player of all time.

There were, however, still peaks to climb. His failure to win the French Open, despite three successive appearances in the final, meant he had yet to complete the fabled and elusive career Grand Slam. Pete Sampras and his 14 major triumphs also cast a shadow over the argument

PREVIOUS PAGE: Federer arrived at Roland Garros in 2009 having lost to Spain's Rafael Nadal in the three previous French Open men's singles finals.

RIGHT: The Swiss battled through to the final in Paris for the fourth time in his career but this time he faced Swede Robin Söderling in the climax of the tournament.

of exactly where the Swiss stood in the tennis pantheon. By the end of 2009, the debate had been settled conclusively.

A five-set defeat to Rafael Nadal in the final of the Australian Open in February, his first defeat in four appearances in the denouement of the tournament in Melbourne, was undoubtedly a bitter pill to swallow. Twice the world number two fought back from a set down to the Spaniard but he could not get over the line in the pivotal fifth set and Nadal served out for his first Australian title. In April, Federer tied the knot with long-time girlfriend, and former tennis pro, Mirka Vavrinec in a secret ceremony in Switzerland but there was precious little time for an extended honeymoon with the French Open in Paris the following month firmly on his horizon.

His initial performances at Roland-Garros were far from convincing. He was taken to four sets by unheralded Argentinean José Acasuso in the second round and then five by Tommy Haas in the fourth round, having to recover from two sets down to dispose of the stubborn German. The big news, however, was Nadal's defeat to Swede Robin Söderling in round four and with the shock elimination of the previously untouchable four-time champion and three-time nemesis of Federer in the final, the Coupe des Mousquetaires was suddenly tantalisingly within reach. The Swiss had to survive another five-set thriller in the last four against Juan Martín del Potro but once he was safely through to a record-equalling 19th major final, he began to dream of a career-defining Parisian triumph. It was Söderling who stood between him and history. The world number 25 had lost all nine of his previous matches against Federer but anyone capable of beating Nadal on clay was a dangerous animal.

The first set lasted just 23 minutes as the Swiss broke the Swede in the first game and stormed to a 6-1 win. The second set was interrupted when a flag-waving spectator confronted Federer on court but once the interloper had been removed, he regained his composure to seal a 2-0 advantage on a tiebreak with four glorious aces. He needed just one more set and broke the Swede again in

game one, surviving break points in the fourth and 10th games before serving out 6-4. "Federer wins the French Open for the first time in his career," declared the Eurosport commentator covering the final, "and in addition must surely

ABOVE: A rapid, straights-sets win over Söderling saw Federer become only the sixth player in the game's history to claim all four Grand Slam titles.

ABOVE: Federer received the French Open trophy from Andre Agassi, the most recent man to record the fabled Major career clean sweep a decade earlier.

be regarded now as the greatest male player of all-time."

Federer had now joined the great names of Fred Perry, Don Budge, Rod Laver, Roy Emerson and, most recently, Andre Agassi as a winner of all four of the majors. To put the achievement into a wider context, the Swiss had done what the likes of Boris Becker and John McEnroe, Ivan Lendl and Jimmy Connors, Björn Borg and Pete Sampras himself had failed to do. With five Wimbledon titles, five US Opens, three Australian Opens and finally the French, he was now also equal to Sampras with 14 career Grand Slam successes.

"The mixed tears of joy and relief ran slowly down Roger Federer's face as he held aloft the Coupe des Mousquetaires having finally won the French Open title in his fourth successive final," said the *Guardian*. "So he became only the sixth man in tennis history to win all four Slam titles, with Andre Agassi, the last man to do it in 1999, presenting him with the trophy. Federer beat Sweden's Robin Söderling 6-1, 7-6 (7-1) and 6-4 in just under two hours and with rain falling for much of the final. As Söderling put Federer's last serve into the net, the Swiss dropped to his knees on clay as if history had suddenly pushed him to ground. And it had."

History, though, waits for no man, not even Federer, and just two weeks after the fairy tale in France he was back in SW19 for Wimbledon for a 11th time in the men's singles and his attempt to surpass Sampras. It was also his chance to

"This was my greatest victory. I can now go the rest of my career without worrying that I would never win the French Open. It takes away so much pressure. Now I can play in peace for the rest of my career. It really wasn't easy to deal with my emotions during the match. Nobody will ever tell me again that I have not won Roland-Garros. It's nice to be up here on the podium as a winner this time. Of course, I'd like to thank Andre [Agassi] for being here. It means the world to me. We've had some great matches over the years. For you to be here, the last man to win all four Grand Slams. Now I know what it really feels like."

Federer *after his historic victory at the 2009 French Open*

RIGHT: The Swiss headed to SW19 in 2009 for the eleventh time aiming to recapture the Wimbledon crown he had surrendered to Rafael Nadal 12 months earlier.

recapture the All England crown after his epic loss to Nadal 12 months earlier.

His procession to a seventh final was almost unblemished. Germany's Philipp Kohlschreiber stole a set in the third round but that lapse aside, Federer was imperious and as the second Sunday of the tournament arrived, he was through to the final to face Andy Roddick for the 21st time in their careers. It was the fourth time the pair had met in the climax of a major and with the Swiss having won all three previous encounters – Wimbledon in 2004 and 2005, and the US Open the following year, dropping just two sets in the process – the pre-match predictions were resoundingly in favour of another comfortable victory for the five-time champion.

The American evidently had other ideas. The first set was locked at 5-5 but when Federer uncharacteristically squandered four break points on the Roddick serve, he was made to rue his profligacy as his opponent closed out 7-5. The second set was equally close and went to a tiebreak but this time it was the sixth seed who would regret his wastefulness, forcing four set points at 6-2, only to allow Federer to reel off six points in succession to win 8-6 and level the match at one apiece. The Swiss's serve was majestic in the third – Roddick took just two points off it – as Federer won another tiebreak 7-5 but Roddick rallied admirably to take the fourth 6-3 and the final, for the third year running, headed uncertainly to a fifth and deciding set. What unfolded next was pure theatre as both men refused to take a backward step and as game after game went with the serve, the match kept the 11 million people in Britain alone watching on television spellbound. The pivotal moment, incredibly, came in the 30th game when Federer was finally able to break the American's serve and, after 95 minutes, the fifth set was settled 16-14 in favour of the Swiss. The 30 games of the deciding set were a new record for a Grand Slam final, comfortably eclipsing the 11-9 scoreline witnessed at the French Open back in 1927.

More significantly, after four hours and 17 minutes of Centre Court drama, Federer now stood alone and unchallenged as the greatest player in major men's singles tennis, with 15 titles. "It's staggering that I've been able to play so well for so many years, staying injury free," he said. "For me to be the player I am now, I'm surprised. I didn't expect it. I never thought I could be this consistent. It's especially nice that so many legends were sitting there - especially Pete [Sampras]. I know how much the record meant to him and he knows how much it means to me. It's not one of those goals you set as a little boy but it's been quite a career and quite a month. This is not why I'm playing tennis, to break records, and this doesn't mean I'm going to stop playing tennis. I hope to come back for many years."

Sampras watched his record fall to the Swiss from the Royal Box on Centre Court. It was his first visit to Wimbledon since 2002 and the American legend was full of praise for the man who had just eclipsed him. "The guy's a legend and now he's an icon," he said. "He's a credit to the game. He can get 17 or 18 majors. If he just keeps it going and stays healthy, he could go to 18, 19, actually. Roger's a friend, he's a great player, he's a good guy."

If Federer thought July could not get any better, he was to be pleasantly surprised. The day after winning Wimbledon for a sixth time in seven years, it was confirmed he had wrestled the ATP number one ranking back from Nadal – which he would retain for the next 48 weeks – while at the end of the month, he became a father for the first time with the birth of twin daughters Myla Rose and Charlene Riva. Losing the final of the US Open to del Potro the following month in five sets, as well as the rebranded year-end ATP World Tour Finals to Nikolay Davydenko, was not in the script but both defeats could not take the gloss of what had been an unforgettable year for Federer both on and off the court.

The next four years saw the Swiss struggle with illness and injury for the first significant time in his career but he was still able to add two more majors to his incredible collection. The first came at the start of 2010 in Australia as he claimed his fourth title in Melbourne. He swept elegantly into the final and in a repeat of the final game in the

OPPOSITE: In a repeat of the finals of both 2004 and 2005, Federer faced American Andy Roddick in the climax of the tournament, dramatically emerging victorious after a five-set epic.

2008 US Open, made short work of Andy Murray to wrap up victory in straight sets. In the process, Federer became only the second father after Agassi to win a Grand Slam. "Guys like Murray have made me a better player," he said after his 6-3, 6-4, 7-6 (13-11) victory. "I think this has been one of my finest performances in a long time, you know, or maybe forever. I really want to try to enjoy the end of my career, because I've reached already so many goals I thought were never possible. I really want to just enjoy the tour, and that's what I'm doing at the moment."

In July, Federer appointed American Paul Annacone, the long-time coach of Sampras, to work with him alongside Severin Lüthi, part of the Swiss Davis Cup set-up, but the new-look coaching team at first struggled to make an impact. A bout of pneumonia did not help matters and although Federer recovered sufficiently to lift the ATP World Tour Finals trophy in London in November for his fifth title, overcoming Nadal 6-3, 3-6, 6-1 in the tournament's new O2 Arena home, 2011 would prove to be a relatively barren year.

There was a fifth appearance in the French Open final to celebrate but for a fourth time Nadal halted his charge at Roland-Garros. Four ATP tour titles were some consolation and after celebrating his 30th birthday in August, he ended the campaign with a record-breaking sixth ATP World Tour Finals triumph, beating France's Jo-Wilfried Tsonga in the final but it was, as ever, more majors that he really craved.

It was apt that it was Wimbledon, his second home, which gave him satisfaction. His run to the 2012 final required the Swiss to overcome world number one Novak Djokovic in the last four but when the Serb was dispatched in four sets on Centre Court, only Murray could prevent him sealing a record-equalling seventh victory at the All England Club. Murray was the first British player to reach the final since 1938 but had lost his two previous Grand Slams to Federer and after three hours and 24 minutes, the Swiss completed the hat-trick over his younger opponent, winning 4-6, 7-5, 6-3, 6-4. Victory saw him dethrone Djokovic as number one in the world and also break Sampras's cumulative record of 286 weeks at the summit of men's tennis – Federer had been one week short of the milestone when he lost the top spot in June 2010.

Back injuries plagued his 2013 campaign and for the first time in 11 years, he failed to reach a major final. At the start of 2014, he once again freshened up his coaching team with the addition of Stefan Edberg but although he made it through to the final of Wimbledon in July, he was beaten in a five-set epic by Djokovic and ultimately ended the season without adding to his tally of 17 majors.

The year was not without joy. In May, Mirka gave birth to the couple's second set of twins, boys Leo and Lenny, and with his young family, his 33rd birthday approaching and his place in the record books already assured, he could have been forgiven for thoughts of a life beyond tennis. Federer, however, was far from finished.

OPPOSITE: Federer's triumph was the sixth All England Club title of his career, leaving The Swiss just one behind Pete Sampras in the Open Era.

FOLLOWING PAGE: Four of the great Wimbledon champions pose together for a shot: Björn Borg, Pete Sampras, Roger Federer and Rod Laver.

DAVIS CUP
WINNER

8

DAVIS CUP WINNER

Triumph at the de-facto annual world championship of men's international tennis, the Davis Cup, had eluded Switzerland for 91 years until Federer inspired his country to a historic maiden victory in 2014 against France.

Roger Federer was just 11-years-old in 1992 when Switzerland reached its first-ever Davis Cup final, 69 years after the nation had made its debut in the competition. Sadly for the Swiss, the USA team they faced at the Tarrant County Centre in Texas contained the formidable quartet of Andre Agassi, Pete Sampras, Jim Courier and John McEnroe, all past or future Grand Slam champions, and the Americans proved too strong for their European opponents on home soil, running out 4-1 winners over the three days of play.

At the time, the young Federer had no idea he would be the man to finally lead the nation to victory in the competition 22 years later. He certainly served a long Davis Cup apprenticeship en route to his moment of glory in 2014 but after 15 seasons without success, even he must have doubted Switzerland would ever become the world champions.

His Davis Cup journey began in 1999 when, as a relatively unknown 17-year-old, he made his international bow on the indoor carpet in Neuchâtel in the World Group stage against Italy. The teenager duly opened his Davis Cup account with a 3-1 win over Davide Sanguinetti in his singles' heat on the first day and although he was beaten in two sets on day three by Gianluca Pozzi in what was a dead rubber, the Swiss claimed the tie 3-2 and progressed to the quarter-finals. Belgium were their opponents in the last eight in Brussels but this time the teenager was outgunned in both his singles matches by older and more experienced opponents, Christophe van Garsse and Xavier Malisse, and Switzerland were knocked out.

Federer made his debut in the doubles the following year alongside Lorenzo Manta, and between 2000 and 2002 made 17 appearances in the competition, winning 14 times. It was, though, in 2003 that Switzerland with Federer in the ranks first demonstrated what they might be capable of as they marched into the semi-finals for only the second time in their history.

The Netherlands were beaten in Arnhem in the first round of the World Group thanks to Federer's straight sets singles wins over Raemon Sluiter and then Sjeng Schalken. Despite still being just 21, he was in even more majestic form in the quarter-finals against France in Toulouse, beating Nicolas Escude in the second rubber of the tie before partnering Marc Rosset in the doubles the following day and registering a 3-1 win against Escude and Fabrice Santoro. He completed a sensational individual weekend with a 6-1, 6-0, 6-2 demolition of Santoro in the fourth rubber and his three points booked Switzerland's place in the last four.

The semi-finals saw the Swiss head down under to face Australia, the 27-time champions,

PREVIOUS PAGE: Federer embarked on Switzerland's bid to lift the Davis Cup in 2014 15 years after making his debut in the tournament as a teenager.

in the Rod Laver Arena in Melbourne. The home side were the overwhelming favourites for the tie but when Federer levelled the match at 1-1 in the second rubber, beating Mark Philippoussis in straight sets in a repeat of that year's Wimbledon final, a potential shock was on the cards. The match was still alive, even though Federer and Rosset lost in the doubles to Wayne Arthurs and Todd Woodbridge and it fell on the young Swiss on the final day to beat Lleyton

Hewitt in the fourth rubber in front of a partisan crowd to prolong proceedings.

Six months older than Federer, Hewitt had two majors to his name compared to his opponent's one when they met in Melbourne in 2003 and the two rising stars of the men's game conjured up a dramatic clash that went all the way to a fifth set. The Swiss took the first set 7-5 and the second 6-2 but the home favourite came roaring back 7-6 and 7-5 and clinched the

BELOW: The 32-year-old Swiss returned to Davis Cup duty in 2014 having missed the previous season's campaign with a persistent back injury.

decisive point Australia needed by winning the fifth 6-1.

Over the next few years, however, Switzerland struggled to make a further, significant impact on the Davis Cup, reaching the last eight of the tournament only once and seven times dropping into the play-off phase of the World Group. All that was to change in 2014 with the timely emergence of a second Swiss tennis heavyweight and Federer's decision to fully commit to the challenge after a number of seasons in which his individual tour schedule had forced him to miss ties.

The 'new' star in the Swiss ranks was Stanislas Wawrinka. The right hander was far from a Davis Cup novice, having made his debut in the competition back in 2004 in a first-round match against Romania in Bucharest, while his triumph in the men's doubles with Federer at the Beijing Olympics in 2008 was an early indicator of his potential. The difference in 2014 was Wawrinka had now finally emerged from Federer's shadow to establish himself as one of the leading lights in the game in his own right.

Wawrinka's big breakthrough came at the Australian Open at the start of the year. Seeded eighth in the men's draw, he marched into the quarter-finals in Melbourne with a sense of real determination and when he dispatched Novak Djokovic, the reigning champion, in a five-set nail-biter, dramatically clinching the final set 9-7, he

PREVIOUS PAGE: Federer and Stan Wawrinka in Davis Cup doubles action against Australia at the Royal Sydney Golf Club in 2011.

sent a seismic shock around the Rod Laver Arena. His victory in the final in four sets over the top seed Rafael Nadal, who had overcome Federer in the last four, was equally unexpected but no less deserved.

All this meant that Switzerland embarked on their bid for Davis Cup glory in 2014 with a newly-crowned Grand Slam champion – only the second Swiss man after Federer to achieve the feat - and a serial major winner in tandem. It also meant Wawrinka began the campaign as the world number three, in sharp contrast to the Olympic year of 2008 when he was ranked down at 28 at the start of the season.

Their challenge began just five days after the climax of the Australian Open against Serbia in the city of Novi Sad. The good news for the Swiss was Djokovic had decided to make himself unavailable for the tie and without their talisman, the Serbian team was able to offer little meaningful resistance. Federer began proceedings with a routine, straight sets win over the world number 268 Ilija Bozoljac in the first rubber. By the end of the first day's play, Switzerland were 2-0 up after Wawrinka had seen off Dušan Lajovic, who was narrowly outside the Top 100, in the second match. Their early advantage meant Switzerland could afford to rest their star duo for the doubles the following day but Marco Chiudinelli and Michael Lammer deputized with distinction and put the tie beyond

ABOVE: Six years after the Swiss pair had famously claimed gold in the men's doubles at the Beijing Olympics, Federer and Wawrinka were reunited in 2014.

Serbia's reach with a four-set win. Federer and Wawrinka took no further part in the match as two dead rubbers were played out on the final day and although Serbia took both points on offer, the Swiss were safely through to the quarter-finals.

The familiar surroundings of Geneva's Palexpo convention centre awaited them for their last four clash with Kazakhstan in early April. This time Wawrinka began proceedings on the first day but was ambushed by Andrey Golubev in four sets and it fell to Federer to level up proceedings with a comfortable three-set victory over Mikhail Kukushkin. The tie was finely balanced but the home crowd were stunned on day two when Wawrinka and Federer renewed their famed Olympic doubles partnership only to lose to Golubev and Aleksandr Nedovesov, and Switzerland found themselves unexpectedly trailing 2-1 heading into the final day.

The sense of anxiety in Geneva was palpably heightened when Wawrinka lost the first set of the opening rubber against Kukushkin. Kazakhstan were just two sets short of a famous result but Wawrinka dug deep and rattled off the next three sets – all of them 6-4 – to keep the hosts in contention. It now all depended on Federer and although the nervousness in the crowd was not allayed when the first set against Golubev went to a tiebreak, he won it 7-0 to go ahead. The next two sets saw him drop just five games as he rattled past his opponent 6-2, 6-3 and in reassuringly rapid time Switzerland were into the semi-finals.

The tournament went into a five-month summer hiatus but reconvened in September in Geneva for the last four showdown with neighbours Italy in what was a local derby. Federer was charged with putting Switzerland on the front foot in the opening rubber and did just that with a 7-6, 6-4, 6-4 win against world number 76 Simone Bolelli and Wawrinka pressed home the advantage later in the day with his own straight sets triumph over Italian number one Fabio Fognini. The Swiss were on a roll but were to regret their decision to rest Federer for the doubles the next day when Wawrinka and Chiudinelli were beaten in five sets by Bolelli and Fognini.

OPPOSITE: The Swiss duo were in imperious form en route to the semi-finals as Serbia in Novi Sad, and then Kazakhstan in Geneva, were eliminated in the early rounds.

As day three approached, the home side still needed one precious point to book their place in the final. Predictably, Federer was sent out first to garner it and he made no mistake as he powered his way to a 6-2, 6-3, 7-6 victory over Fognini to establish an unassailable 3-1 lead in the tie.

The Swiss crowd erupted as the 33-year-old completed his mission and Federer was carried around the court on the shoulders of Wawrinka and team captain Severin Luthi in celebration. "It's nice sharing the emotions with your fans and team members," he said, as he looked ahead to facing France in the final. "It was a pretty quick court, so if you're not serving so well, there are always going to be errors – it wasn't the best performance for either of us. Some of the best

match-ups I've had have been against France, but we're very pleased to be in the final. After the difficult defeat [in the semi-final] in 2003, we had another chance this year."

Switzerland's build-up to the final was far from serene. Having played all three of their previous Davis Cup ties on hard courts, there were already lingering concerns about how the side would adapt to the clay of the Stade Pierre-Mauroy in Lille. But such worries were eclipsed when, just six days before the start of the final, Federer sustained a back injury. It happened, ironically, playing against Wawrinka in the semi-finals of the ATP World Tour Finals in London and, although he was able to battle through the pain to overcome his Davis Cup teammate in straight sets, it was

BELOW: The final of the 2014 Davis Cup saw Switzerland travel to Lille to face nine-time champions France on the indoor clay courts of the Stade Pierre-Mauroy.

sufficiently serious to stop him contesting the final against Djokovic the following day and he headed to Lille with a genuine question mark over his ability to compete.

"Even if Switzerland win both first-day singles – Federer is not certain to play in the reverse singles on Sunday," reported the *Guardian*. "Sources say he was not exactly moving like an angel on the practice court. Should Federer's back give out on him again during the final, France would become favourites to lift the trophy."

The man himself was more upbeat about the situation but acknowledged that France, the nine-time champions, most recently in 2001, would be the sternest test of the Swiss so far. "I've had back pain many times in my life, in my career, not only in the last few years, but also back in junior days," he said. "I can definitely draw from some experience. I know what's possible and what's not. I know how much I can push. Obviously, if I'm stepping out on the court, that means I can play. It's a difficult match regardless. If I were 100 per cent, it would be tough in itself because of the crowd, because of the opponent. There's a lot of question marks for everybody, including myself."

Some of those questions were initially answered when Wawrinka took to the court to play Jo-Wilfried Tsonga, the world number 12, in the opening rubber. The Swiss demolished his opposite number 6-1 in the first set and although the Frenchman levelled up after taking the second 6-3, Wawrinka was in no mood for a protracted encounter and rattled off the next two sets 6-3 and 6-2 to give Switzerland first blood in the match. Federer was next up against Gaël Monfils, 18th in the ATP rankings, but a second Swiss win failed to materialize as the 33-year-old struggled with the effects of his injury and the Frenchman levelled the tie with alarming ease in straight sets.

It was a nervous 24 hours for the Swiss camp but the following day, Federer emerged to partner Wawrinka in the doubles and now appeared reborn as they dismantled the French duo of Julien Benneteau and Richard Gasquet. The first set was wrapped up 6-3 and, although the home pairing made the visitors work harder in the second and

OPPOSITE: The Swiss suffered a shock defeat to Gaël Monfils in the singles on the opening day of the final but bounced back on day two in the doubles to edge Switzerland into a 2-1 lead.

ABOVE: Federer beat Richard Gasquet in straight sets on day three to give the Swiss an unassailable 3-1 advantage and his country a maiden Davis Cup success.

third, there was no coming back and the Swiss completed a crucial 6-3, 7-5, 6-4 victory that put them on the verge of a maiden Davis Cup triumph.

It was now France's turn to suffer misfortune when it was revealed Tsonga could not play in the day three singles rubbers due to an arm injury. His withdrawal saw Gasquet drafted in to face Federer in the first, potentially decisive match and in front of a vociferous crowd of 27,448 inside the cavernous Stade Pierre-Mauroy – a world record

for a competitive tennis match – the 17-time Grand Slam winner came out in pursuit of history.

Gasquet had lost 12 of his 14 previous meetings with Federer, although his two victories had both come on clay, but from the start of the match the Frenchman appeared intimidated by the man on the opposite side of the net. Federer dropped just four points on serve en route to securing the first set 6-4 and he was even more dominant in the second, running out a 6-2 winner. One more set was

court in the ATP World Tour Finals against Novak Djokovic. Federer had injured his back in the semi-final against Davis Cup teammate Stan Wawrinka during a hard-fought contest. Flash to Sunday: Federer, his back healed, teary with joy, his right arm resting on Wawrinka's shoulder as the Swiss national anthem played."

The BBC tennis correspondent Russell Fuller wrote after Switzerland's win: "It was Tsonga's elbow, rather than Federer's back, which proved the weak link in the end. Federer's ruthless but straightforward victory seemed inevitable as Gasquet is not a man who enjoys playing on Roland-Garros's main court, let alone in front of a world record crowd with the hopes of a nation on his shoulders. This has been another triumph for Federer – whose collection could now be considered complete – but also for Wawrinka, who played as well in the final week of the season as he did in winning the Australian Open at the very start."

Federer's contribution to the cause in 2014 was exceptional. In total, he played seven singles rubbers, winning six, and won one of the two doubles matches he contested. Wawrinka was the rock on which the Swiss challenge was built, with his four victories in the singles and that one doubles success, but it was Federer who provided the extra firepower at the pivotal moments through what was a victorious campaign.

He returned to the Swiss Davis Cup fold in 2015 to help the side beat the Netherlands in the World Group play-offs in Geneva in September, winning both his singles rubbers. To date, that was his last appearance for his country in the competition as he sought to manage his schedule, protect his body and prolong his career.

He remains, nonetheless, the most successful Swiss player in Davis Cup history. None of his compatriots past or present can match his 40 victories in 48 singles rubbers, nor his overall tally of 52 wins in 70 combined singles and doubles matches, while his 15-year-long career in the tournament is a record only equalled by Heinz Günthardt, who was part of the Swiss team between 1976 and 1990.

all Switzerland required and Federer duly delivered in emphatic style, registering another 6-2 scoreline to seal a famous victory.

"Tennis's rhythm of weekly tournaments means fortunes sink or soar with unrelenting regularity," said *USA Today*. "But even among those customary highs and lows, Roger Federer's last seven days stand out. A week ago, the 33-year-old Swiss appeared in warm-up gear at London's O2 Arena and somberly told fans that he could not take the

"This one is for the boys. This is not for me, I have won enough. I am just happy we can give everyone in our country a historic moment. Stan has put in so much effort over the years. He played an unbelievable weekend and that is what gave me the opportunity today. I think it's an amazing day for sports in our country, in Switzerland, We're a smaller country. We don't win bigger events every other week. So, from that standpoint, I think it's a big day. It was definitely one of the better feelings in my career, no doubt about it."

Federer *reflects on Switzerland's Davis Cup triumph.*

OPPOSITE: Switzerland's historic Davis Cup triumph was built on Federer's six wins from seven single rubbers over the course of a dominant campaign.

EPIC
RIVALRIES

9

EPIC RIVALRIES

The gladiatorial nature of tennis frequently elevates the sport to another level and during Federer's record-breaking 20-year career, the Swiss has crossed swords with some of the game's all-time greats.

PREVIOUS PAGE: Federer's epic, era-defining rivalry with Spain's Rafael Nadal began when the pair first met in the Last 32 of the Miami Open in 2004.

In terms of the number of competing players, the ATP tour boasts a sizeable entourage but there has inevitably always been a smaller cadre of serial title challengers, the men who regularly play their way through to the business end of tournaments and, ultimately, silverware. Federer is the preeminent among them but in his two decades in the professional ranks, he has enjoyed a succession of fierce and enthralling rivalries with challengers to his crown.

The first true heavyweight rival he repeatedly faced was Andre Agassi. The great American showman, winner of eight Grand Slams, met the young Swiss only 11 times – four of them in majors – but their brief encounters were symbolic of the changing of the guard as Agassi's generation edged towards retirement and Federer's rose to prominence. Agassi was victorious in all three of their opening matches, the first in the Swiss Indoors in Federer's home town of Basel in 1998. But once the Swiss had opened his account at the Masters Cup in Houston five years later, it was one-way traffic to underline the sense of the game's changing landscape.

Their greatest clash came in 2004 in the quarter-finals of the US Open at Flushing Meadows. Federer was the top seed with three majors to his name, Agassi the sixth seed, and the pair produced a pulsating spectacle that the Swiss closed out 6-3 in the fifth set. They met again in the final of the same tournament the following year but this time it took Federer, the defending champion, only four sets to overcome his 35-year-old opponent and lift his sixth Grand Slam trophy. Agassi retired in 2006 with a 3-8 losing record against the Swiss.

The next potential usurper was Lleyton Hewitt. The Australian turned professional in 1998, the same year as Federer, but with his pugnacious, aggressive demeanour and less fluid technique he was in many ways the stylistic antithesis of his rival. The two men had met on the junior circuit back in 1996 but it was three years later at the Grand Prix de Tennis de Lyon that they

renewed acquaintances as fully-fledged pros, the Australian emerging the winner from their last 32 clash two sets to one.

Hewitt dominated proceedings in their early exchanges, winning seven of their first nine matches, which included a dramatic win from two sets down in the semi-finals of the Davis Cup in 2003, a remarkable fightback that eliminated

ABOVE: The Swiss and Andre Agassi played an exhibition match 220 meters above sea level on the top of the Burj Al Arab hotel in Dubai in 2005.

OPPOSITE: Federer and Agassi faced each other 11 times in their careers, most notably in the final of the 2005 US Open.

Switzerland from the competition and propelled Australia to the final and, ultimately, the title. The tide, however, turned the following year when they played for the first time in a Grand Slam, Federer claiming victory in four sets in the last 16 of the Australian Open in front of Hewitt's home crowd. It was the start of the Swiss's growing superiority and he would go on to beat Hewitt in 15 of their next 17 showdowns.

There was just one Grand Slam final clash between the pair, the denouement of the US Open in 2004. Federer was targeting his first title in New York, while Hewitt was hoping to repeat his 2001 Flushing Meadows triumph but the match proved surprisingly one-sided as the Swiss smashed the Australian 6-0, 7-6, 6-0 in record time. The result had a depressing sense of déjà vu for Hewitt, who lost to his nemesis five times in majors between

2004 and 2005. On each occasion, Federer went on to lift the trophy.

The erstwhile doubles partners – they reached the third round of Wimbledon together in 1999 – played for the last time in the final of the Brisbane International in 2014 in their 27th career clash, 15 years after their first encounter. Hewitt took the honours two sets to one to end their rivalry with a small degree of satisfaction but it was scant consolation for the seven from seven major defeats the Swiss had already inflicted on him.

Hot on the heels of Hewitt came Andy Roddick, who first went up against Federer in 2001, but if the Australian suspected the Swiss had something of a Grand Slam hoodoo over him, the American was convinced of it after losing four times in the final of a major. The fascinating element of this latest rivalry was that Roddick was the first top player, unlike Agassi and Hewitt, who possessed a serve with the power to genuinely challenge the Swiss on the faster hard and grass courts. That Federer was consistently able to find a return, despite the pace and weight of Roddick's delivery, was the decisive factor in their 24 matches, the platform for the Swiss's winning 21-3 record and, ultimately, the catalyst for the American's beleaguered observation that "I'm gonna have to start winning some matches to call it a rivalry".

Their opening clash came in Federer's backyard of Basel in the 2011 Swiss Indoors, where the home favourite took the honours. Roddick opened his account at the Canadian Open two years later, but it was their head-to-head record in Grand Slams, as well as the fact that Federer dethroned Roddick as the world number one in early 2004, that ultimately defined their dynamic. The American had won the 2003 US Open title but his hopes of adding another major to his CV were comprehensively dashed with victories for Federer in the 2004 and 2005 Wimbledon finals, as well as at the US Open in 2006. There was one last chance of redemption with the climax of Wimbledon in 2009 but it was tears of dismay rather than joy at the end of a marathon contest, with Federer winning 16-14 in the fifth set, which lasted an incredible and record-breaking hour and 35 minutes.

The next chapter in the story of Federer's greatest rivalries is not of one new challenger but three, with the emergence of Rafael Nadal, Andy Murray and Novak Djokovic in the mid-to-late 2000s. Tennis now had a "Big Four" rather than one singularly dominant player and the Swiss found himself increasingly under attack on multiple fronts.

Spain's Nadal was the first of the trio to lay down the gauntlet, following their maiden

BELOW: Federer's 2009 Wimbledon final against Andy Roddick, culminating in a dramatic 16-14 win in the fifth set, is widely regarded as one of the greatest matches in tennis history.

meeting at the 2004 Miami Open. For many tennis devotees, their rivalry is the greatest the sport has ever produced, eclipsing even that of John McEnroe and Ivan Lendl, Boris Becker and Stefan Edberg or Björn Borg and Jimmy Connors.

The tale of the tape confirms the essential nature of their rivalry and their respective affinity with different surfaces. In their 38 clashes [to the end of September 2018], Federer leads Nadal 13-10 on hard or grass courts but on his beloved clay the Spaniard enjoys a 13-2 winning record.

Such was the stark contrast in fortunes when they clashed, depending on the court, that in Majorca in 2007 they played an exhibition match dubbed "The Battle of the Surfaces" on which Federer played on a turfed side of the net while Nadal was opposite on clay. "The idea really appeals to me as we both dominate one of the surfaces," the Swiss said. "Rafa holds the record of 72 victories in series on clay and I have not been defeated on grass since 48 matches." For the record, the Spaniard edged the three-set contest on a third set tiebreak.

The more weighty issue of Grand Slam titles has seen the pair clash nine times in major finals. The first two occasions were in 2006 with Nadal victorious on the Parisian clay, only for Federer to exact his revenge on the grass in SW19 a few weeks later. It was the same story the following year when the Spaniard successfully defended his French crown and the Swiss was triumphant at Wimbledon. In 2008, however, there was a shift in the balance of power. Nadal predictably made it a hat-trick of wins at Roland-Garros but Federer's widely anticipated reply at Wimbledon failed to materialize and the Spaniard beat him in a five-set epic on Centre Court, more than once voted the greatest match in history, to become the All England champion for the first time. The 2009 Australian Open final similarly went the distance and also to Nadal, as did the French two years later, but in their most recent encounter in 2018, it was Federer who came out on top, claiming a fifth Australian crown after taking the fifth and decisive set 6-3.

OPPOSITE: Federer and Nadal have met in a record nine Grand Slam finals, the first coming in 2006 at Roland Garros in the climax of the French Open.

"Roger is an amazing champion. If he's playing very good, I have to play unbelievable. It's impossible, especially when he's playing with good confidence. When he's 100 per cent, he's playing in another league. It's impossible to stop him. If anyone says I am better than Roger, then he doesn't know anything about tennis. Everybody likes to say that Roger is the greatest player of all time because it's so nice to watch him play. He is the best player in history, no other player has ever had such quality."

Rafael Nadal *on Federer*

PREVIOUS PAGE: The Swiss's enduring and dramatic rivalry with Nadal has been characterised by the players' respective dominance on the grass of Wimbledon and Parisian clay.

126 | EPIC RIVALRIES

The duo have also exchanged pleasantries three times in the end-of-season ATP World Tour Finals, the game's unofficial fifth major. The Swiss was victorious first time out, beating Nadal 6-3, 3-6, 6-1 in the final at London's O2 Arena in 2010 and repeated the trick the following year in the round robin stage. In 2013, however, it was the Spaniard's turn, knocking out his perennial rival in the semi-finals.

The battle to be ranked number one in the world by the ATP has added an extra dimension to their relationship over the years. Federer holds the record for the most cumulative weeks on top (310) and the longest single reign as top dog (237) but the two have vied constantly for the crown. It was the Spaniard who deposed the Swiss in August 2008, only for Federer to return the favour in July the following year. In total, Nadal has displaced Federer five times at the pinnacle of the ATP list, while Federer has toppled Nadal on four separate occasions. "I'm his number one fan," Federer said of Nadal in 2017. "I think his game is simply tremendous. He's an incredible competitor and I'm happy we've had some epic battles in the past."

Britain's Murray was the next of the big three to throw his hat into the challengers' ring when he faced the world number one in the final of the Thailand Open in Bangkok in 2005. Federer closed out a 2-0 victory in their inaugural clash but it was just the start of an intense battle between the pair

BELOW: The final of the men's singles at the London 2012 Olympics at Wimbledon was the 17th time Federer and Andy Murray had faced each other.

RIGHT: Federer and Novak
Djokovic first contested a
Grand Slam final at the US
Open in 2007, a clash the Swiss
won at Flushing Meadows in
straight sets.

that would eventually see Murray become one of only three men to register 10 or more career victories against the great man.

Sadly for the Brit, none of those wins came in their first four Grand Slam meetings. The first three matches were major finals – the 2008 US Open, the 2010 Australian Open and Wimbledon 2012 – but Murray did finally end his Slam drought in 2013 when he beat Federer in five sets in the semi-finals in Melbourne. A year later, the Swiss redressed the balance at the Rod Laver Arena with victory in the last eight. Federer also proved too strong in 2015 when they met in SW19 for a second time, booking his place in another final in straight sets.

Wimbledon, however, was the scene for Murray's most memorable match against the Swiss – the final of the 2012 London Olympics. Federer already had a gold medal from the doubles in Beijing four years earlier but his hopes of doubling his collection were dashed by the home favourite at the All England Club, courtesy of a crushing 6-2, 6-1, 6-4 victory.

Last but not least came Djokovic and an intriguing rivalry that has swung one way and then another over the years since their maiden meeting in Monte Carlo in 2006. That neither player has ever registered more than four consecutive wins over the other tells its own story and, unlike Federer's dynamic with Nadal, it has been one played out by two men who both prefer to venture out on hard courts and grass rather than on the comparatively soporific clay.

That they hold the record for the most head-to-head matches in Grand Slam history with 15 merely adds to the epic nature of their ongoing tussle. The vagaries of the ranking system dictated that 10 of those 15 games have come at the semi-final stage of a major. Federer has won three to Djokovic's seven and the Serb also holds the advantage at clashes in a quartet of Slam finals. The first of the four was back in 2007 when the Swiss was too strong for the third seed at the US Open, running out a straight sets winner. 2014 and 2015 saw Djokovic make amends with back-to-back Wimbledon triumphs and a cathartic win at the US Open.

The Serb, therefore, has the edge in Grand Slams but their overall career head-to-head reveals the constant, tight battle the two have enjoyed, arguably because of their mutual affinity for fast courts and similar styles. Djokovic, up until the end of September 2018, was narrowly ahead with 24 wins to his rival's 22 but it was noteworthy that 15 of their perennially dramatic 46 career games had required a deciding set to settle matters.

ABOVE: The Swiss and the Serb's long-standing rivalry has seen both men register victories over the other in each of the four Grand Slam tournaments.

A REMARKABLE RENAISSANCE

RENAISSANCE

10

A **REMARKABLE** RENAISSANCE

Longevity at elite level is increasingly rare in the unrelenting world of modern, professional sport, but in 2017 and then again in 2018, Federer demonstrated that age and two decades on the ATP tour had done nothing to diminish his legendary powers.

When Roger Federer won the Wimbledon title in 2012 at the age of 30, equalling Pete Sampras's record of seven SW19 men's singles crowns, some thought it would be the final time the great Swiss would lift a Major trophy. Sampras had been 31 when he won his last Grand Slam – the 2002 US Open – but with the emergence of Rafael Nadal and Novak Djokovic as the new powerhouses in the game, it seemed the Swiss's star was irrevocably on the wane.

His results in 2015, in the wake of the euphoria over Switzerland's Davis Cup success, appeared to lend weight to the argument. A third-round exit at the Australian Open, followed by a quarter-final defeat in the French in Paris was below par by his own previously phenomenal standards, and although he did reach the Wimbledon and US Open finals, he was beaten on both occasions by Djokovic, six years his junior, in four sets. The guard, it appeared, was changing and Federer would have to be content with his record haul of 17 Slams.

There was little that unfolded in 2016 to dispel the feeling that the Swiss was in terminal, albeit still effortlessly elegant decline and no longer the force of old. Djokovic once again proved too strong for him over four sets in the semi-final of the Australian Open and when he was beaten in the last four at Wimbledon by Canadian Milos Raonic, the world number seven, there was a growing

acceptance among even his most devoted fans that he was slipping further behind. Back and knee injuries did not help his cause – the former keeping him out of the French Open and ending his record of 65 consecutive appearances at Grand Slam tournaments dating back to his Roland-Garros debut 17 years ago. A knee injury led to surgery for the first time in his career, forcing him to miss the US Open. The stark facts were that he finished the season at a lowly 16th in the rankings and without winning an ATP title for the first time since the distant days of 2000.

It was then more in hope than expectation that Federer arrived in Melbourne in January 2017 for the 18th Australian Open of his career, looking for a fifth title. He was seeded a lowly 17th for the

competition and although he eased through the early rounds without any undue alarms, by the time the fourth round arrived, he was facing higher-ranked players. It was time, according to recent form and reputation, for his tournament to come to an end.

Federer proceeded to make a mockery of the theory. In the last 32, he dispatched the fifth seed, Japan's Kei Nishikori in a five-set thriller and in the quarter-finals he beat Mischa Zverev of Germany in straight sets. The fourth seed and compatriot Stan Wawrinka was his next victim in the last four after another five-set epic, and against the odds the Swiss was through to the final in Melbourne.

For the ninth time, Federer would face Nadal in the climax of a major in what was also a repeat of

BELOW: Victory in five dramatic sets over the Spaniard gave the Swiss his 18th Major title and revenge for his defeat in the final eight years earlier.

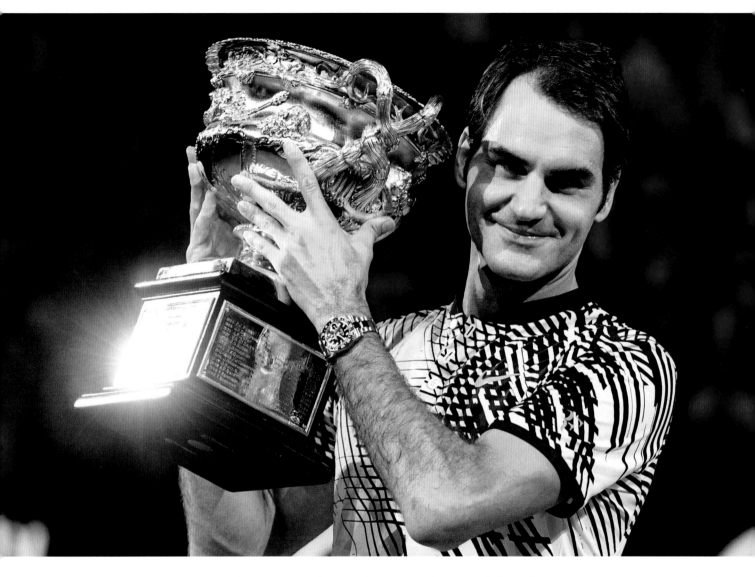

ABOVE: Federer's emotional triumph in Melbourne at the age of 35 was his fifth Australian Open crown and proof his glittering career was far from finished.

their showdown in Melbourne eight years earlier. The Spaniard had won six of their eight previous Grand Slam finals, including their 2009 meeting at the Rod Laver Arena. Given the Swiss's recent struggles and fitness issues and that the Australian Open was his first tournament since Wimbledon the previous summer, Nadal was the favourite to bring the Federer revival to an abrupt halt.

Perhaps inevitably, two of the game's greatest-ever rivals conspired to conjure up an undisputed classic. The first set went Federer's way, dropping only four points on serve en route to a 6-4 scoreline, only for Nadal to display his trademark pugnacity in the second and take it 6-3. The Swiss edged in front, comfortably winning the third 6-1 with two breaks, but the Spaniard was up to the task and levelled once again in the fourth, taking a breathless contest into a deciding fifth set. An early break saw Nadal storm into a 3-1 lead, only for Federer to gloriously roll back the years, win five games on the spin and take the fifth 6-3 after three hours and 37 minutes of pulsating action.

"I've been coming here for almost 20 years now and I've always enjoyed it, and now my family does too," Federer said after lifting his 18th major, five years after securing his 17th. "Thanks again for everything, to everybody. I hope to see you next year. If not, this was a wonderful run here and I can't be more happy to win. Tennis is a tough sport. There are no draws. If there were, I would have been happy to accept one and share it with Rafa. Everybody says they work very hard - I do the same - but I try not to shout about it. I'd like to thank my team. It's been a different last six months. I didn't think I'd make it but here I am."

At 35, Federer was two years younger than the legendary Australian Ken Rosewall had been when he claimed his home title in 1972. Even though he was not the oldest ever winner of the crown, the tennis media were in doubt about the significance of the veteran's victory in the autumn of his career.

"Of course it was going to go to five sets," wrote the BBC's Tom Fordyce. "Of course it was going to make you feel sick for four hours. Of course it was going to go places that no other final and no other players could possibly go. Before this Australian Open final between Roger Federer and Rafael Nadal even began, it felt like the Beatles reforming in 1979 for a one-off gig. When Federer's forehand finished it, deep into the Melbourne night, it was as if they had released a new Revolver too. Federer, supposed to be not only past his prime but past the period when he was past his prime, took on logic, his nemesis and the unarguable passing of time. In coming past all three he may have pulled off not only the best of his 18 Grand Slam singles titles but possibly the greatest Slam victory of all."

It was tempting for the rejuvenated Swiss to have launched headlong into a challenge for a second French Open title later in the year. But discretion was the better of valour and he announced he was to sidestep Roland-Garros, as well as the entire clay court season, in order to protect his body and focus all his energies on Wimbledon. It was to prove a wise decision.

The Swiss was seeded third at the All England Club and, in a reflection of his Lazarus-like return to the pinnacle of the game after Melbourne, he was

once again seen by the majority as the favourite for a tournament he had not won in five years. Federer clearly revelled in such public confidence and did not drop a set as he charged into his 11th final in SW19, where he faced Croatia's Marin Cilic for an eighth time and the fourth in majors. Sadly, the prospect of a meaningful contest on Centre Court evaporated due to a debilitating blister on Cilic's left foot – he broke down in tears in the second set as he struggled to move freely – but Federer could ill afford sympathy for his stricken opponent until the match was over and, watched by wife Mirka and his four children, charged to a one-sided 6-3, 6-1, 6-4 victory in just an hour and 41 minutes.

"It is very special to win eight titles," he said. "Wimbledon was always my favourite tournament, and will always be my favourite tournament. My heroes walked the grounds here. Because of them I think I became a better player too. And number eight obviously means a lot to me because to be part of Wimbledon history is truly amazing. I think the younger twins think this is a nice view and a nice playground - hopefully, one day they'll understand. They come for the finals. It's a wonderful moment for the family and my team. This one is for us. Thank you to Wimbledon, thank you Switzerland."

ABOVE: Federer's family were on hand at Wimbledon in the summer of 2017 to witness his bid to secure a record eighth All England Club title.

RIGHT: The Swiss's straight sets victory over Marin Cilic on Centre Court saw his surpass Pete Sampras and William Renshaw as the most successful men's player in Wimbledon history.

Not for the first time in his career, the incredible Swiss set a whole new raft of new records that day. At 35 years and 11 months old, he became the oldest Wimbledon champion of the Open Era. His eighth All England crown set him apart from both Pete Sampras and 19th-century pioneer William Renshaw, both with seven singles titles, as the most successful man in the long and illustrious history of the game's oldest Grand Slam tournament. He also became the first player since Björn Borg in 1976 to lift the trophy without losing a single set. His 11th appearance in the final was a record, as was what was his 70th appearance in a Grand Slam tournament. His third-round victory over Mischa Zverev of Germany was his 317th in Grand Slam singles, eclipsing the 316 milestone of Serena Williams to make it the most prolific male or female player in majors history.

A quarter-final loss to Juan Martin del Potro and a semi-final reverse against David Goffin in the ATP World Tour Finals back in London represented a low-key end to the year, but there was still no diminishing the extent to which 2017 had been a staggering rebirth for the Swiss. It was the first season since 2009 he had won multiple Grand Slams and his haul of seven titles was his best in a decade. His overall win-loss ratio of 52-5 was his strongest record in 11 years.

The sense of anticipation in tennis as Federer prepared for the 2018 campaign was palpable. All eyes turned to Melbourne and the Australian Open and the burning question was whether 2017 had been a glorious but fleeting swansong or whether he could maintain his unprecedented comeback.

He quickly provided an unequivocal answer, sweeping aside opponent after opponent in straight sets in Australia as he swept imperiously into the final. He was, in truth, aided by the retirement of South Korean Chung Hyeon towards the end of the second set in the last four but the match was already firmly in his grasp when his opponent was forced off, and he was through to the final Down Under for a seventh time. It was Cilic again who awaited him but unlike their meeting at Wimbledon seven months earlier, the 29-year-old Croat was now unencumbered by a foot injury and physically ready to mount a credible challenge.

The first set, however, was something of a procession for Federer, who won the opening four games and finished it off with consecutive aces. Neither player could affect a break in the second and Cilic took it 7-5 on the tiebreak but the Swiss reasserted himself in the third and ran out a 6-3 winner. The fourth set saw Federer squander two break points in the fourth game and when the Croat broke his serve for the first time in the match en route to winning the set 6-3, the final was destined to go all the way. A break in the second game for the Swiss appeared to shatter Cilic's dream of a famous fightback and in the end the defending champion was untroubled when it really mattered, clinching the set 6-1 for the title.

"Roger Federer has never been one to hide his emotions and the 36-year-old Swiss was in floods of tears here on Sunday after becoming the first man in history to win 20 Grand Slam titles," wrote Paul Newman in the *Independent*. "At the presentation ceremony, Federer struggled to get through his speech after beating Marin Cilic 6-2, 6-7, 6-3, 3-6, 6-1 to win the Australian Open for the sixth time. Federer famously broke down in tears here after losing to Rafael Nadal in the 2009 final – his only defeat in his record seven appearances in the final - and was again overcome by emotion here. A remarkable standing ovation followed as the whole stadium rose to applaud Federer for several minutes while the big screens showed the tears rolling down his face. The greatest player of all time was made to work for his latest triumph but if anyone had any doubts as to whether he could repeat his extraordinary feats of last year, when he won two Grand Slam titles upon his return from a six-month break because of injury, they were surely erased here."

Once again, his Australian exploits required a rapid updating of some of the game's long-standing records. The first male ever to reach 20

majors, he joined the greats of the women's game Margaret Court, Serena Williams and Steffi Graf as only one of four players to reach the milestone, while the gap of 14 years, six months and 23 days between winning Wimbledon in 2003 and success in Melbourne in 2018 was the longest between major victories in Open Era history. At the age of 36 years and 173 days when he beat Cilic, he became only the fourth man in the Open Era to win four Grand Slams in his 30s. His triumph inside the Rod Laver Arena was also an unprecedented 10th successful defence of a major title in his career.

Perhaps inevitably, questions about just how long the champion could maintain his remarkable defiance of the years followed his final win. "I don't think age is an issue, per se," he replied. "It's just a number. I've won three Slams now in 12 months. I can't believe it myself. I've just got to keep a good schedule, stay hungry, then maybe good things can happen. But I need to be very careful in my planning, really decide beforehand what are my goals, what are my priorities. I think that's what's going to dictate how successful I will be moving forward. But I'm happy I'm in that position right now."

The year was not to yield a 21st major – the closest he came was a quarter-final appearance at Wimbledon – but there was further cause for celebration in February when he won his 97th ATP tour title in Rotterdam, a result which propelled him back to the summit of the rankings for the fourth time in his career. At 36, he became the oldest man to be recognized as world number one and by the end of 2018, after two more brief stints at the top, he had spent a record 310 weeks as the game's undisputed best player.

Exactly what the future holds for Federer is difficult to predict. What is evident is that those who were writing his sporting obituary as he moved into his 30s have been proved premature and if his age-defying displays in 2017 and 2018 were any guide, it would be unwise to bet against him lifting another Grand Slam trophy. There will inevitably come a day when the iconic Swiss does finally pack away his racket for the last time but it does not appear imminent.

ABOVE: A record-breaking Wimbledon title and a 20th Grand Slam overall: even Federer could scarcely have imagined this just a couple of years earlier.

"Roger Federer stands tallest of all as Wimbledon's history man. With a record eighth title at the All England club and a 19th Grand Slam success, achieved without losing a set, the 35-year-old remains a class apart. Victory meant the Swiss master, who turns 36 next month, surpassed the big-serving American 'Pistol' Pete Sampras and the Victorian-era great William Renshaw, who claimed seven. What made this victory more remarkable still was that the era when Federer's racket played like a Stradivarius [...] had appeared over for good last year."

Sean Ingle *in the Guardian*

OPPOSITE: Victory over Cilic in the Rod Laver Arena was the 30th appearance in a Grand Slam final of Federer's career, 15 years after his first Major trophy.

CAREER
STATISTICS

JUNIOR SINGLES RECORD

1996

Tournament	Date	Opponent	Result
Swiss Junior Tournament – Davos, Switzerland	15–21 July	Nathan Healey (AUS)	Won – Last 16 – 7-6, 4-6, 4-6
World Youth Cup Final – Switzerland	10–14 September	Lleyton Hewitt (AUS) Febi Widhiyanto (INA) Vijay Kannan (IND) Nahuel Fracassi (ITA)	Won – Main Draw – 4-6, 7-6, 6-4 Lost – Play-Off – 5-7, 7-5, 5-7 Won – Play-Off – 6-0, 7-6 Won –Play-Off – 3-6, 6-3, 6-1
Sunshine Cup Final – Florida, USA	December	Petr Kralert (CZE) Adrian Garcia (CHL) Balazs Vaci (HUN) Han-Hui Tsai (TPE)	Lost – Round Robin – 6-1, 0-6, 1-6 Won – Round Robin – 5-7, 6-2, 6-2 Lost – Round Robin – 5-7, 2-6 Won – Round Robin – 6-3, 6-0
Casablanca Cup – Tlanepantla, Mexico	22–28 December	Sebastien Aickele (GER)	Lost – Last 32 – 6-7, 6-3, 5-7
Coffee Bowl – San Jose, Costa Rica	30 December – 5 January	Diego Ayala (USA)	Lost – Last 16 – 4-6, 1-6

RIGHT: Federer's Junior Wimbledon triumph in 1998, beating Irakli Labadze in straight sets in the final, was an early indication of the teenager's huge potential.

1997

Tournament	Date	Opponent	Result
International Junior Championships of Venezuela – Caracas, Venezuela	6–12 January	Jerome Haehnel (FRA)	Lost – Last 64 – 2-6, 4-6
City of Florence International Tournament – Florence, Italy	24–30 March	Davide Bramanti (ITA)	Lost – Last 64 – 4-6, 6-3, 6-7
Prato International Junior Tournament – Florence, Italy	5–11 May	Luka Kutanjac (CRO)	Won – Final – 6-4, 6-0
Italian Junior Championships – Milan, Italy	19–24 May	Rodolfo Rake (PER)	Lost – Quarter-Final – 1-6, 4-6
Eddie Herr International Junior Championships – Florida, USA	8–14 December	Edgardo Massa (ARG)	Lost – Last 64 – 3-6, 4-6

1998

Tournament	Date	Opponent	Result
Victorian Junior Championships – Victoria, Australia	9–14 January	Julien Jeanpierre (FRA)	Won – Final – 6-4, 6-4
Australian Harcourt Junior Championships – Melbourne, Australia	18–24 January	Julien Jeanpierre (FRA)	Lost – Semi-Final – 1-6, 4-6
Australian Open Juniors – Melbourne, Australia	26 January – 1 February	Andreas Vinciguerra (SWE)	Lost – Semi-Final – 6-4, 5-7, 5-7
City of Florence International Tournament – Florence, Italy	8–13 April	Filippo Volandri (ITA)	Won – Final – 7-6, 6-3
Italian Junior Open – Milan, Italy	18–24 May	Jerome Haehnel (FRA)	Lost – Last 32 – 6-4, 5-7, 2-6
Belgian International Junior Championships – Charleroi, Belgium	25–30 May	Bob Borella (DEN)	Lost – Quarter-Final – retired
French International Junior Championships – Paris, France	31 May – 7 June	Jaroslav Levinsky (CZE)	Lost – Last 64 – 4-6, 7-5, 7-9
LTA International Junior Championships – Roehampton, England	21–26 June	Taylor Dent (USA)	Lost – Semi-Final – 6-7, 6-4, 3-6
Wimbledon Juniors – Wimbledon, England	27 June – 5 July	Irakli Labadze (GEO)	Won – Final – 6-4, 6-4
European Closed Junior Championships – Klosters, Switzerland	20–26 July	Feliciano López (ESP)	Lost – Semi-Final – 6-4, 2-6, 4-6
US Open Juniors – New York, USA	31 May – 7 June	David Nalbandian (ARG)	Lost – Final – 3-6, 5-7
Eddie Herr International Junior Championships – Florida, USA	30 November – 6 December	Eric Prodon (FRA)	Lost – Last 16 – 4-6, 6-3, 3-6
Orange Bowl Championships – Florida, USA	13–20 December	Guillermo Coria (ARG)	Lost – Semi-Final – 7-5, 6-3

SENIOR SINGLES RECORD

2001

Tournament	Date	Opponent	Surface	Result
Milan Indoor – Milan, Italy	29 January – 4 February	Julien Boutter FRA)	Carpet	6-4, 6-7, 6-4

2002

Tournament	Date	Opponent	Surface	Result
Sydney International – Sydney, Australia	7–13 January	Juan Ignacio Chela (ARG)	Outdoor/Hard	6-3, 6-3
German Open – Hamburg, Germany	13–19 May	Marat Safin (RUS)	Outdoor/Clay	6-1, 6-3, 6-4
Vienna Open – Vienna, Austria	7–13 October	Jiri Novak (CZE)	Indoor/Hard	6-4, 6-1, 3-6, 6-4

2003

Tournament	Date	Opponent	Surface	Result
Marseille Open – Marseille, France	10–16 February	Jonas Björkman (SWE)	Indoor/Hard	6-2, 7-6
Dubai Championships – Dubai, UAE	24 February – 2 March	Jiri Novak (CZE)	Outdoor/Hard	6-1, 7-6
Bavarian International – Munich, Germany	28 April – 4 May	Jarkko Nieminen (FIN)	Outdoor/Clay	6-1, 6-4
Halle Open – Halle, Germany	9–15 June	Nicolas Kiefer (GER)	Outdoor/Grass	6-1, 6-3
Wimbledon – Wimbledon, England	23 June – 6 July	Mark Philippoussis (AUS)	Outdoor/Grass	7-6, 6-2, 7-6
Vienna Open – Vienna, Austria	6–12 October	Carlos Moya (SPA)	Indoor/Hard	6-3, 6-3, 6-3
Masters Cup – Texas, USA	10–16 November	Andre Agassi (USA)	Outdoor/Hard	6-3, 6-0, 6-4

2004

Tournament	Date	Opponent	Surface	Result
Australian Open – Melbourne, Australia	19 January – 1 February	Marat Safin (RUS)	Outdoor/Hard	7-6, 6-4, 6-2
Dubai Championships – Dubai, UAE	1–7 March	Feliciano Lopez (SPA)	Outdoor/Hard	4-6, 6-1, 6-2
Indian Wells Masters – California, USA	8–21 March	Tim Henman (GBR)	Outdoor/Hard	6-3, 6-3
German Open – Hamburg, Germany	10–16 May	Guillermo Coria (ARG)	Outdoor/Clay	4-6, 6-4, 6-2, 6-3
Halle Open – Halle, Germany	6–13 June	Mardy Fish (USA)	Outdoor/Grass	6-0, 6-3

2004 *continued*

Wimbledon – Wimbledon, England	21 June – 4 July	Andy Roddick (USA)	Outdoor/Grass	4-6, 7-5, 7-6, 6-4
Swiss Open – Gstaad, Switzerland	5–11 July	Igor Andreev (RUS)	Outdoor/Clay	6-2, 6-3, 5-7, 6-3
Canadian Open – Toronto, Canada	26 July – 1 August	Andy Roddick (USA)	Outdoor/Hard	7-5, 6-3
US Open – New York, USA	30 August – 9 September	Lleyton Hewitt (AUS)	Outdoor/Hard	6-0, 7-6, 6-0
Thailand Open – Bangkok, Thailand	27 September – 3 October	Andy Roddick (USA)	Indoor/Hard	6-4, 6-0
Masters Cup – Texas, USA	15–21 November	Lleyton Hewitt (USA)	Outdoor/Hard	6-2, 6-2

2005

Tournament	Date	Opponent	Surface	Result
Qatar Open – Doha, Qatar	3–9 January	Ivan Ljubicic (CRO)	Outdoor/Hard	6-3, 6-1
Rotterdam Open – Rotterdam, Holland	14–20 February	Ivan Ljubicic (CRO)	Indoor/Hard	5-7, 7-5, 7-6
Dubai Championships – Dubai, UAE	21–27 February	Ivan Ljubicic (CRO)	Outdoor/Hard	6-1, 6-7, 6-3
Indian Wells Masters – California, USA	7–20 March	Lleyton Hewitt (AUS)	Outdoor/Hard	6-2, 6-4, 6-4
Miami Open – Miami, USA	21 March – 3 April	Rafael Nadal (SPA)	Outdoor/Hard	2-6, 6-7, 7-6, 6-3, 6-1
German Open – Hamburg, Germany	9–15 May	Richard Gasquet (FRA)	Outdoor/Clay	6-3, 7-5, 7-6
Halle Open – Halle, Germany	6–12 June	Marat Safin (RUS)	Outdoor/Grass	6-4, 6-7, 6-4
Wimbledon – Wimbledon, England	20 June – 3 July	Andy Roddick (USA)	Outdoor/Grass	6-2, 7-6, 6-4
Cincinnati Masters – Cincinnati, USA	15–21 August	Andy Roddick (USA)	Outdoor/Hard	6-3, 7-5
US Open – New York, USA	29 August – 11 September	Andre Agassi (USA)	Outdoor/Hard	6-3, 2-6, 7-6, 6-1
Thailand Open – Bangkok, Thailand	26 September – 2 October	Andy Murray (GBR)	Outdoor/Hard	6-3, 7-5

2006

Tournament	Date	Opponent	Surface	Result
Qatar Open – Doha, Qatar	2–8 January	Gael Monfils (FRA)	Outdoor/Hard	6-3, 7-6
Australian Open – Melbourne, Australia	16–29, January	Marcos Baghdatis (CYP)	Outdoor/Hard	5-7, 7-5, 6-0, 6-2
Indian Wells Masters – California, USA	6–19 March	James Blake (USA)	Outdoor/Hard	7-5, 6-3, 6-0
Miami Open – Miami, USA	20 March – 3 April	Ivan Ljubicic (CRO)	Outdoor/Hard	7-6, 7-6, 7-6
Halle Open – Halle, Germany	12–18 June	Tomas Berdych (CZE)	Outdoor/Grass	6-0, 6-7, 6-2
Wimbledon – Wimbledon, England	26 June – 9 June	Rafael Nadal (SPA)	Outdoor/Grass	6-0, 7-6, 6-7, 6-3
Canadian Open – Toronto, Canada	7–13 August	Richard Gasquet (FRA)	Outdoor/Hard	2-6, 6-3, 6-2
US Open – New York, USA	28 August – 10 September	Andy Roddick (USA)	Outdoor/Hard	6-2, 4-6, 7-5, 6-1

Japan Open – Tokyo, Japan	2–8 October	Tim Henman (GBR)	Outdoor/Hard	6-3, 6-3
Madrid Open – Madrid, Spain	16–22 October	Fernando Gonzalez (CHL)	Indoor/Hard	7-5, 6-1, 6-0
Swiss Indoors – Basel, Switzerland	23–29 October	Fernando Gonzalez (CHL)	Carpet	6-2, 6-2, 7-6
Masters Cup – Shanghai, China	13–19 November	James Blake (USA)	Indoor/Hard	6-0, 6-3, 6-4

2007

Tournament	Date	Opponent	Surface	Result
Australian Open – Melbourne, Australia	15–28 January	Fernando Gonzalez (CHL)	Outdoor/Hard	7-6, 6-4, 6-4
Dubai Championships – Dubai, UAE	26 February – 4 April	Mikhail Youzhny (RUS)	Outdoor/Hard	6-4, 6-3
German Open – Hamburg, Germany	14–20 May	Rafael Nadal (SPA)	Outdoor/Clay	2-6, 6-2, 6-0
Wimbledon – Wimbledon, England	25 June – 8 July	Rafael Nadal (SPA)	Outdoor/Grass	7-6, 4-6, 7-6, 2-6, 6-2
Cincinnati Masters – Cincinnati, USA	13–19 August	James Blake (USA)	Outdoor/Hard	6-1, 6-4
US Open – New York, USA	27 August – 9 September	Novak Djokovic (SER)	Outdoor/Hard	7-6, 7-6, 6-4
Swiss Indoors – Basel, Switzerland	22–28 October	Jarkko Nieminen (FIN)	Indoor/Hard	6-3, 6-4
Masters Cup – Shanghai, China	12–18 November	David Ferrer (SPA)	Indoor/Hard	6-2, 6-3, 6-2

2008

Tournament	Date	Opponent	Surface	Result
Estoril Open – Oeiras, Portugal	14–20 April	Nikolay Davydenko (RUS)	Outdoor/Clay	7-6, 1-2 retired
Halle Open – Halle, Germany	9–15 June	Philipp Kohlschreiber (GER)	Outdoor/Grass	5-7, 7-5, 6-0, 6-2
US Open – New York, USA	25 August – 7 September	Andy Murray (GBR)	Outdoor/Hard	6-2, 7-5, 6-2
Swiss Indoors – Basel, Switzerland	20–26 October	David Nalbandian (ARG)	Indoor/Hard	6-3, 6-4

2009

Tournament	Date	Opponent	Surface	Result
Madrid Open – Madrid, Spain	11–17 May	Rafael Nadal (SPA)	Outdoor/Clay	6-4, 6-4
French Open – Paris, France	25 May – 7 June	Robin Soderling (SWE)	Outdoor/Clay	6-1, 7-6, 6-4
Wimbledon – Wimbledon, England	22 June – 5 July	Andy Roddick (USA)	Outdoor/Grass	5-7, 7-6, 7-6, 3-6, 16-14
Cincinnati Masters – Cincinnati, USA	17–23 August	Novak Djokovic (SER)	Indoor/Hard	6-1, 7-5

2010

Tournament	Date	Opponent	Surface	Result
Australian Open – Melbourne, Australia	15–28 January	Andy Murray (GBR)	Outdoor/Hard	6-3, 6-4, 7-6
Cincinnati Masters – Cincinnati, USA	16–22 August	Mardy Fish (USA)	Outdoor/Hard	6-7, 7-6, 6-4
Stockholm Open – Stockholm, Sweden	18–24 October	Florian Mayer (GER)	Indoor/Hard	6-4, 6-3
Swiss Indoors – Basel, Switzerland	1–7 November	Novak Djokovic (SER)	Indoor/Hard	6-4, 3-6, 6-1
World Tour Finals – London, England	22–28 November	Rafael Nadal (SPA)	Indoor/Hard	6-3, 3-6, 6-1

2011

Tournament	Date	Opponent	Surface	Result
Qatar Open – Doha, Qatar	3–8 January	Nikolay Davydenko (RUS)	Outdoor/Hard	6-3, 6-4
Swiss Indoors – Basel, Switzerland	31 October – 6 November	Kei Nishikori (JPN)	Indoor/Hard	6-1, 6-3
Paris Masters – Paris, France	7–13 November	Jo-Wilfriend Tsonga (FRA)	Indoor/Hard	6-1, 7-6
World Tour Finals – London, England	21–27 November	Jo-Wilfriend Tsonga (FRA)	Indoor/Hard	6-3, 6-7, 6-3

RIGHT: Federer was the undisputed king of Centre Court between 2003 and 2007, claiming five successive Wimbledon crowns at the All England Club.

2012

Tournament	Date	Opponent	Surface	Result
Rotterdam Open – Rotterdam, Netherlands	13–19 February	Juan Martin del Potro (ARG)	Indoor/Hard	6-1, 6-4
Dubai Championships – Dubai, UAE	27 February – 3 March	Andy Murray (GBR)	Outdoor/Hard	7-5, 6-4
Indian Wells Masters – California, USA	5–18 March	John Isner (USA)	Outdoor/Hard	7-6, 6-3
Madrid Open – Madrid, Spain	7–13 May	Tomas Berdych (CZE)	Outdoor/Clay	3-6, 7-5, 7-5
Wimbledon – Wimbledon, England	25 June – 8 July	Andy Murray (GBR)	Outdoor/Grass	4-6, 7-5, 6-3, 6-4
Cincinnati Masters – Cincinnati, USA	13–19 August	Novak Djokovic (SER)	Outdoor/Hard	6-0, 7-6

2013

Tournament	Date	Opponent	Surface	Result
Halle Open – Halle, Germany	10–16 June	Mikhail Youzhny (RUS)	Outdoor/Grass	6-7, 6-3, 6-4

2014

Tournament	Date	Opponent	Surface	Result
Dubai Championships – Dubai, UAE	24 February – 1 March	Tomas Berdych (CZE)	Outdoor/Hard	3-6, 6-4, 6-3
Halle Open – Halle, Germany	9–15 June	Alejandro Falla (COL)	Outdoor/Grass	7-6, 7-6
Cincinnati Masters – Cincinnati, USA	11–17 August	David Ferrer (SPA)	Outdoor/Hard	6-3, 1-6, 6-2
Shanghai Masters – Shanghai, China	6–12 October	Gilles Simon (FRA)	Outdoor/Hard	4-6, 7-5, 6-3, 6-4
Swiss Indoors – Basel, Switzerland	20–26 October	David Goffin (BEL)	Indoor/Hard	6-2, 6-2

2015

Tournament	Date	Opponent	Surface	Result
Brisbane International – Brisbane, Australia	5–11 January	Milos Raonic (CAN)	Outdoor/Hard	6-4, 6-7, 6-4
Dubai Championships – Dubai, UAE	23–28 February	Novak Djokovic (SER)	Outdoor/Hard	6-3, 7-5
Istanbul Open – Istanbul, Turkey	27 April – 3 May	Pablo Cuevas (URU)	Outdoor/Clay	6-3, 7-6
Halle Open – Halle, Germany	15–21 June	Andreas Seppi (ITA)	Outdoor/Grass	7-6, 6-4
Cincinnati Masters – Cincinnati, USA	17–23 August	Novak Djokovic (SER)	Outdoor/Hard	7-6, 6-3
Swiss Indoors – Basel, Switzerland	26 October – 1 November	Rafael Nadal (SPA)	Indoor/Hard	6-3, 5-7, 6-3

2017

Tournament	Date	Opponent	Surface	Result
Australian Open – Melbourne, Australia	16–29 January	Rafael Nadal (SPA)	Outdoor/Hard	6-4, 3-6, 6-1, 3-6, 6-3
Indian Wells Masters – California, USA	6–19 March	Stan Wawrinka (SUI)	Outdoor/Hard	6-4, 7-5
Miami Open – Miami, USA	20 March – 2 April	Rafael Nadal (SPA)	Outdoor/Hard	6-3, 6-4
Halle Open – Halle, Germany	19–25 June	Alexander Zverev (GER)	Outdoor/Grass	6-1, 6-3
Wimbledon – Wimbledon, England	3–16 July	Marin Cilic (CRO)	Outdoor/Grass	6-3, 6-1, 6-4
Shanghai Masters – Shanghai, China	9–15 October	Rafael Nadal (SPA)	Outdoor/Hard	6-4, 6-3
Swiss Indoors – Basel, Switzerland	23–29 October	Juan Martin del Potro (ARG)	Indoor/Hard	6-7, 6-4, 6-3

2018

Tournament	Date	Opponent	Surface	Result
Australian Open – Melbourne, Australia	16–29 January	Rafael Nadal (SPA)	Outdoor/Hard	6-4, 3-6, 6-1, 3-6, 6-3
Indian Wells Masters – California, USA	6–19 March	Stan Wawrinka (SUI)	Outdoor/Hard	6-4, 7-5
Miami Open – Miami, USA	20 March – 2 April	Rafael Nadal (SPA)	Outdoor/Hard	6-3, 6-4
Halle Open – Halle, Germany	19–25 June	Alexander Zverev (GER)	Outdoor/Grass	6-1, 6-3
Wimbledon – Wimbledon, England	3–16 July	Marin Cilic (CRO)	Outdoor/Grass	6-3, 6-1, 6-4
Shanghai Masters – Shanghai, China	9–15 October	Rafael Nadal (SPA)	Outdoor/Hard	6-4, 6-3
Swiss Indoors – Basel, Switzerland	23–29 October	Juan Martin del Potro (ARG)	Indoor/Hard	6-7, 6-4, 6-3

OLYMPIC RECORD

SYDNEY 2000

Format	Date	Opponent	Result
Singles	18 September – 1 October	David Prinosil (GER) Karol Kucera (SVK) Mikael Tillstrom (SWE) Karim Alami (MAR) Tommy Haas (GER) Arnaud di Pasquale (FRA)	Won – Last 64 – 6-2, 6-2 Won – Last 32 – 6-4, 7-6 Won – Last 16 – 6-1, 6-2 Won – Quarter-Final – 7-6, 6-1 Lost – Semi-Final – 3-6, 2-6 Lost – Bronze Play-Off – 6-7, 7-6, 3-6

ATHENS 2004

Format	Date	Opponent	Result
Singles	16–22 August	Nikolay Davydenko (RUS) Tomas Berdych (CZE)	Won – Last 64 – 6-3, 5-7, 6-1 Lost – Last 32 – 6-4, 5-7, 5-7
Doubles (with Yves Allegro)	16–22 August	M Fyrstenberg & M Matkowski (POL) M Bhupathi & L Paes (IND)	Won – 1st Round – 6-2, 6-2 Lost – 2nd Round – 2-6, 6-7

BEIJING 2008

Format	Date	Opponent	Result
Singles	11–17 August	Dmitry Tursunov (RUS) Rafael Arevalo (ESA) Tomas Berdych (CZE) James Blake (USA)	Won – Last 64 – 6-4, 6-2 Won – Last 32 – 6-2, 6-4 Won – Last 16 – 6-3, 7-6 Lost – Quarter-Final – 4-6, 6-7
Doubles (with Stan Wawrinka)	11–17 August	S Bolelli & A Seppi (ITA) D Tursunov & M Youzhny (RUS) M Bhupathi & L Paes (IND) B Bryan & M Bryan (USA) S Aspelin & T Johansson (SWE)	Won – Last 32 – 7-5, 6-1 Won – Last 16 – 6-4, 6-3 Won – Quarter-Final – 6-2, 6-4 Won – Semi-Final – 7-6, 6-4 Won – Final – 6-3, 6-4, 6-7, 6-3

LEFT: The Swiss made his third Olympic appearance at the Beijing Games in 2008 and won gold with Stan Wawrinka in the men's doubles.

LONDON 2012

Format	Date	Opponent	Result
Singles	30 July – 5 August	Alejandro Falla (COL) Julien Benneteau (FRA) Denis Istomin (UZB) John Isner (USA) Juan Martin del Potro (ARG) Andy Murray (GBR)	Won – Last 64 – 6-3, 5-7, 6-3 Won – Last 32 – 6-2, 6-2 Won – Last 16 – 7-5, 6-3 Won – Quarter-Finals – 6-4, 7-6 Won – Semi-Final – 3-6, 7-6, 19-17 Lost – Final – 2-6, 1-6, 4-6
Doubles (with Stan Wawrinka)	30 July – 5 August	K Nishikori & G Soeda (JAP) J Erlich & A Ram (ISR)	Won – Last 32 – 6-7, 6-4, 6-4 Lost – Last 16 – 6-1, 6-7, 3-6

DAVIS CUP RECORD

1999

Stage	Format	Opponent	Result
World Group 1st Round v Italy	Singles	Davide Sanguinetti Gianluca Pozzi	Won – 6-4, 6-7, 6-3, 6-4 Lost – 4-6, 6-7
World Group Quarter-Finals v Belgium	Singles	Christophe van Garsse Roger Malisse	Lost – 6-7, 6-3, 6-1, 5-7, 1-6 Lost – 6-4, 3-6, 5-7, 6-7

2000

Stage	Format	Opponent	Result
World Group 1st Round v Australia	Singles Doubles (with L Manta)	Mark Philippoussis Lleyton Hewitt W Arthurs & Stolle Sandon	Won – 6-4, 7-6, 4-6, 6-4 Lost – 2-6, 6-3, 6-7, 1-6 Won – 3-6, 6-3, 6-4, 7-6
World Group Play-Off v Belarus	Singles Doubles (with L Manta)	Vladimir Voltchkov Roger Malisse M Mirnyi & V Voltchkov	Won – 4-6, 7-5, 7-6, 5-7, 6-2 Lost – 2-6, 6-3, 6-7, 1-6 Won – 2-6, 7-6, 7-5, 7-6

2001

Stage	Format	Opponent	Result
World Group 1st Round v USA	Singles Doubles (with L Manta)	Martin Todd Jan-Michael Gambill J-M Gambill & J Gimelstob	Won – 6-4, 7-6, 4-6, 6-1 Won – 7-5, 6-2, 4-6, 6-2 Won – 6-4, 6-2, 7-5
World Group Quarter-Finals v France	Singles Doubles (with L Manta)	Nicolas Escude Arnaud Clement C Pioline & F Santoro	Lost – 4-6, 7-6, 3-6, 4-6 Won – 6-4, 3-6, 7-6, 6-4 Won – 5-7, 6-3, 7-6, 6-7, 9-7

2002

Stage	Format	Opponent	Result
World Group 1st Round v Russia	Singles Doubles (with M Rosset)	Marat Safin Yevgeny Kafelnikov Kafelnikov & M Safin	Won – 7-5, 6-1, 6-2 Won – 7-6, 6-1, 6-1 Lost – 2-6, 6-7, 7-6, 2-6
World Group Play-Off v Morocco	Singles Doubles (with G Bastl)	Hicham Arazi Younes El Aynaoui K Alami & Y El Aynaoui	Won – 6-3, 6-2, 6-1 Won – 6-3, 6-2, 6-1 Won – 6-4, 6-1, 6-4

2003

Stage	Format	Opponent	Result
World Group 1st Round v Netherlands	Singles	Raemon Sluiter	Won – 6-2, 6-1, 6-3
		Sjeng Schalken	Won – 7-6, 6-4, 7-5
	Doubles (with G Bastl)	P Haarhuis & M Verkerk	Lost – 6-3, 3-6, 4-6, 5-7
World Group Quarter-Finals v France	Singles	Nicolas Escude	Won – 6-4, 7-5, 6-2
		Fabrice Santoro	Won – 6-1, 6-0, 6-2
	Doubles (with M Rosset)	N Escude & F Santoro	Won – 6-4, 3-6, 6-3, 7-6
World Group Semi-Finals v Australia	Singles	Mark Philippoussis	Won – 6-3, 6-4, 7-6
		Lleyton Hewitt	Lost – 7-5, 6-2, 6-7, 5-7, 1-6
	Doubles (with M Rosset)	W Arthurs & T Woodbridge	Lost – 6-4, 6-7, 7-5, 4-6, 4-6

2004

Stage	Format	Opponent	Result
World Group 1st Round v Romania	Singles	Victor Hanescu	Won – 7-6, 6-3, 6-1
		Andrei Pavel	Won – 6-3 6-2, 7-5
	Doubles (with Y Allegro)	A Pavel & G Trifu	Won – 6-4, 1-6, 6-3, 3-6, 10-8
World Group Quarter-Finals v France	Singles	Nicolas Escude	Won – 6-2, 6-4, 6-4
		Arnaud Clement	Won – 6-2, 7-5, 6-4
	Doubles (with Y Allegro)	N Escude & M Llodra	Lost – 7-6, 3-6, 6-7, 3-6

2005

Stage	Format	Opponent	Result
World Group Play-Off v Great Britain	Singles	Alan Mackin	Won – 6-0, 6-0, 6-2
	Doubles (with Y Allegro)	G Rusedski & A Murray	Won – 7-5, 2-6, 7-6, 6-2

2006

Stage	Format	Opponent	Result
World Group Play-Off v Serbia & Montenegro	Singles	Janko Tipsarevic	Won – 6-3, 6-2, 6-2
		Novak Djokovic	Won – 6-3, 6-2, 6-3
	Doubles (with Y Allegro)	I Bozoljac & N Zimonjic	Won – 7-6, 6-4, 6-4

2007

Stage	Format	Opponent	Result
World Group Play-Off v Czech Republic	Singles	Radek Stepanek	Won – 6-3, 6-2, 6-7, 7-6
		Tomas Berdych	Won – 7-6, 7-6, 6-3
	Doubles (with Y Allegro)	T Berdych & R Stepanek	Lost – 6-3, 7-5, 6-7, 4-6, 4-6

2008

Stage	Format	Opponent	Result
World Group Play-Off v Belgium	Singles Doubles (with S Wawrinka)	Kristof Vliegen X Malisse & O Rochus	Won – 7-6, 6-4, 6-2 Won – 4-6, 7-6, 6-3, 6-3

2009

Stage	Format	Opponent	Result
World Group Play-Off v Italy	Singles	Simone Bolelli Potito Starace	Won – 6-3, 6-4, 6-1 Won – 6-3, 6-0, 6-4

2011

Stage	Format	Opponent	Result
Group One Quarter-Finals v Portugal	Singles Doubles (with S Wawrinka)	Rui Machado F Gil & L Tavares	Won – 5-7, 6-3, 6-4, 6-2 Won – 6-3, 6-4, 6-4
World Group Play-Off v Australia	Singles Doubles (with S Wawrinka)	Lleyton Hewitt Bernard Tomic C Guccione & L Hewitt	Won – 5-7, 7-6, 6-2, 6-3 Won – 6-2, 7-5, 3-6, 6-3 Lost – 6-2, 4-6, 2-6, 6-7

2012

Stage	Format	Opponent	Result
World Group 1st Round v USA	Singles Doubles (with S Wawrinka)	John Isner M Bryan & M Fish	Lost – 6-4, 3-6, 6-7, 2-6 Lost – 6-4, 3-6, 3-6, 3-6
World Group Play-Off v Netherlands	Singles Doubles (with S Wawrinka)	Thlemo De Bakker Robin Haase R Haase & J-J Roger	Won – 6-3, 6-4, 6-4 Won – 6-1, 6-4, 6-4 Lost – 4-6, 2-6, 7-5, 3-6

2014

Stage	Format	Opponent	Result
World Group 1st Round v Serbia	Singles	Ilija Bozoljac	Won – 6-4, 7-5, 6-2
World Group Quarter-Finals v Kazakhstan	Singles Doubles (with S Wawrinka)	Mikhail Kukushkin Andrey Golubev A Golubev & A Nedovyesov	Won – 6-4, 6-4, 6-2 Won – 7-6, 6-2, 6-3 Lost – 4-6, 6-7, 6-4, 6-7
World Group Semi-Finals v Italy	Singles	Simone Bolelli Fabio Fognini	Won – 7-6, 6-4, 6-4 Won – 6-2, 6-3, 7-6

2014 *continued*

World Group Final v France	Singles	Gael Monfils	Lost – 1-6, 4-6, 3-6
		Richard Gasquet	Won – 6-4, 6-2, 6-2
	Doubles (with S Wawrinka)	J Benneteau & R Gasquet	Won – 6-3, 7-5, 6-4

2015

Stage	Format	Opponent	Result
World Group Play-Off v Netherlands	Singles	Jesse Huta Galung	Won – 6-3, 6-4, 6-3
		Thlemo De Bakker	Won – 6-3, 6-2, 6-4
	Doubles (M Chiudinelli)	T De Bakker & M Middelkoop	Lost – 6-7, 6-4, 6-4, 4-6, 1-6

LEFT: After 13 previous unsuccessful challenges, Federer finally lifted the Davis Cup with Switzerland in 2014 after beating France in the final.

PICTURE CREDITS

The publishers would like to thank the following sources for their kind permission to reproduce the pictures in this book.

GETTY IMAGES: /AELTC: 98-99, 138; /AFP: 4-5; /Ron C Angle: 32; /Al Bello: 50-51; /Torsten Blackwood/AFP: 58-59; /Clive Brunskill: 3, 15, 18-19, 21, 33, 35, 60, 61, 80, 82-83, 84-85, 96-97, 124-125, 136-137, 160; /Simon Bruty/Sports Illustrated: 122-123; /David Cannon: 119; /Jean Catuffe: 114, 159; /Denis Charlet/AFP: 110-111; /Lorenzo Ciniglio/Corbis: 128; /Tim Clayton/Corbis: 10-11, 129, 130-131, 135; /Thomas Coex/AFP: 12-13; /Fabrice Coffrini/AFP: 106-107, 108L, 108-109; /Phil Cole: 56-57; /Frank Coppi/Popperfoto: 36-37, 40-41; /Carl Court/AFP: 127; /Paul Crock/AFP: 133R; /Adrian Dennis/AFP: 92-93; /Julian Finney: 78-79, 100-101, 105, 112-113, 152; /Frederick Florin/AFP: 22; /Gamma-Rapho: 74; /Paul Gilham: 94-95; /Mike Hewitt: 25, 26; /Tommy Hindley/Professional Sport/Popperfoto: 23, 71, 155; /Findlay Kember/AFP: 62; /Saeed Khan/AFP: 132-133, 140-141, 143; /Matt King: 104, 120; /Pierre Lahalle/TempSport/Corbis/VCG: 75; /Bob Martin/Sports Illustrated: 86-87; /Leo Mason/Popperfoto: 46-47; /Chris McGrath: 68-69; /Jason Merritt: 9; /Jason Nevader: 54; /Peter Parkes/AFP: 139; /Philippe Perusseau/Icon Sport: 76; /Ryan Pierse: 64-65, 89, 90, 116-117, 151; /Popperfoto: 66-67; /Professional Sport/Popperfoto: 28-29, 43, 53, 63, 146; /Michael Regan: 144-145; /Roberto Schmidt/AFP: 72-73; /Ezra Shaw: 48-49; /Howard Earl Simmons/NY News Archive: 118; /Matthew Stockman: 39, 88, 121; /TPN: 6-7; /William West/AFP: 103, 134; /Greg Wood/AFP: 44-45

SHUTTERSTOCK: /Luca Bruno/AP/REX: 34; /Keystone/REX: 31

Every effort has been made to acknowledge correctly and contact the source and/or copyright holder of each picture and Carlton Books Limited apologises for any unintentional errors or omissions that will be corrected in future editions of this book.

RIGHT: Federer shares a laugh with fellow pros Andy Murray, Jamie Murray and Tim Henman during a charity even in Glasgow, in 2017.